WHAT READERS ARE SAYING ABOUT GEORGE MACDONALD'S *Your Life in Christ*:

"I am reading through for the third time *Your Life in Christ*. Please continue to edit and print your insights as it most assuredly fills a need for me. Obedience is not a popular idea. Sonship is not a popular idea. I really relish MacDonald's writings and your comments."

—Dave Black

"I am grateful to have discovered you, and because of you, George MacDonald. I read about him in *Surprised by Joy* and was aware of *Unspoken Sermons* . . . but reading "The Creation in Christ" was an experience unlike other reading—with the promise of more to come. . . . I'm sure I can spend the rest of my life endeavoring to allow God to make real in my life the truths and insights of this one book, *Your Life in Christ*. Thank you in the fullest possible sense."

—Jerrel Kee

Books by Michael Phillips

Is Jesus Coming Back As Soon As We Think?
Destiny Junction • *Kings Crossroads*
Make Me Like Jesus • *God, A Good Father*
Jesus, An Obedient Son
Best Friends for Life (with Judy Phillips)
George MacDonald: Scotland's Beloved Storyteller
Rift in Time • *Hidden in Time*
Legend of the Celtic Stone • *An Ancient Strife*
Your Life in Christ (George MacDonald)
The Truth in Jesus (George MacDonald)

AMERICAN DREAMS
Dream of Freedom • *Dream of Life*

THE SECRET OF THE ROSE
The Eleventh Hour • *A Rose Remembered*
Escape to Freedom • *Dawn of Liberty*

THE SECRETS OF HEATHERSLEIGH HALL
Wild Grows the Heather in Devon
Wayward Winds
Heathersleigh Homecoming
A New Dawn Over Devon

SHENANDOAH SISTERS
Angels Watching Over Me
A Day to Pick Your Own Cotton
The Color of Your Skin Ain't the Color of Your Heart
Together Is All We Need

CAROLINA COUSINS
A Perilous Proposal • *The Soldier's Lady*
Never Too Late

GEORGE MacDONALD

EDITED BY MICHAEL PHILLIPS

THE TRUTH IN JESUS

THE NATURE OF TRUTH AND HOW WE COME TO KNOW IT

BETHANYHOUSE

Minneapolis, Minnesota

The Truth in Jesus
Copyright © 2006
Michael Phillips

Cover design by Jennifer Parker
Cover painting: *Upper Sacramento River* by Julian Walbridge Rix

Scripture quotations are as MacDonald used them, from The Authorized Version,
1611, and the Revised Version, 1885.

Published by Bethany House Publishers
11400 Hampshire Avenue South
Bloomington, Minnesota 55438

Bethany House Publishers is a division of
Baker Publishing Group, Grand Rapids, Michigan.

Printed in the United States of America

ISBN-13: 978-0-7642-0154-7
ISBN-10: 0-7642-0154-9

Library of Congress Cataloging-in-Publication Data

MacDonald, George, 1824–1905.
    The truth in Jesus : the nature of truth and how we come to know it / George
MacDonald ; edited by Michael Phillips.
        p.   cm.
    ISBN-13: 978-0-7642-0154-7 (pbk. : alk. paper)
    ISBN-10: 0-7642-0154-9 (pbk. : alk. paper)
    1. Truth—Religious aspects—Christianity. I. Phillips, Michael R., 1946- II.
Title.
    BT50.M243   2006
    230—dc22   2006019699

CONTENTS

INTRODUCTION

When a man recognized as perhaps the most influential Christian author of the twentieth century speaks of his spiritual "master," one might naturally assume the elder to be as well known as his protégé. Curiously, this has never been the case in the spiritual relationship between C. S. Lewis (1898–1963) and George MacDonald (1824–1905). Though Lewis persistently pointed to MacDonald not only as the man whose writings began his own pilgrimage out of atheism toward Christianity but also as his lifelong literary spiritual mentor, the name and writings of MacDonald have remained in relative obscurity, comprising but a footnote in most Lewis studies.

Millions of readers the world over are fascinated with and enamored by Lewis's ideas, spiritual perspectives, and method of communication. Yet few seem curious about where his outlooks and insights and his wide-ranging breadth as a writer and thinker came from.

How did C. S. Lewis *become* the man he was?

The answer is a simple one, and we have it from his own lips. He became the man he was, the Christian he was, the writer he was, from learning at George MacDonald's feet.

From MacDonald he learned faith, he learned doctrine, he learned obedience, he learned a perspective on Scripture, he learned of God's character, he learned the power of communicating through fiction and fairy tale. This is not to say that Lewis would not have been a literary force in his own right. But MacDonald's influence is so pervasive through his thought and writings that it is impossible to separate Lewis's own gifts from their roots. He credits MacDonald as foundational in every book he ever wrote.

With this series, begun in 2005 to commemorate the centenary of George MacDonald's death, modern readers are presented for the first time with newly formatted editions of MacDonald's powerful nonfiction, drawn mostly from his volumes of *Unspoken Sermons*, about which Lewis commented, "My own debt to this book is almost as great as one man can owe to another." It is my sincere hope and prayer that these editions will exercise an impact in the lives of their readers equal to that of these ideas in the life of C. S. Lewis. For MacDonald's life-changing message is one that must be told anew to every generation. The call of his life and the essential cry of his heart through the body of his work is a call to a knowledge of God's truth, a call to a lifestyle of simplicity and obedience, and a call for Christians to step into their destiny as the sons and daughters of a good and loving Father.[1]

---

[1]For additional background on MacDonald and Lewis, see the Introduction to *Your Life in Christ*, the first book in this series (Minneapolis: Bethany House, 2005); on MacDonald himself, see Michael Phillips, *George MacDonald: A Biography of Scotland's Beloved Storyteller* (Minneapolis: Bethany House, 2005, reissue edition).

The editing of the selections that follow in *The Truth in Jesus* is as minimal as I have been able to make it. However, extracting the ore from MacDonald's writings does require some effort. There are those who take exception to the idea of "editing" another's work at all. But the fact that MacDonald's nineteenth-century originals are cumbersome seems justification enough. There may be some who do not find them so, but I am not one of them. I find them difficult. Thus my goal is to make his wisdom and prophetic insight about God readable and graspable to anyone willing to put in the effort to understand his groundbreaking and occasionally controversial ideas. It is my hope that the minimal editing I have employed with these writings will help you discover these rich veins within MacDonald's thought.

This is not to say, even now, that this will be a light read. MacDonald's ideas and processes of thought are occasionally so profound that nothing makes them easy. We are not used to having to think quite so hard for our spiritual food. We live in a superficial age where doctrinal formula and personal experience are the parameters by which spirituality is judged.

MacDonald's outlook and approach do take some getting used to. I find that many passages require two or three readings. But I also find spiritual gold awaiting me, sometimes buried deep but always ready to shine out brilliantly from the page when suddenly I *see* it.

Some may still wonder why such editing is necessary. For two reasons: the complex progression of MacDonald's ideas, and the elaborately entangled grammatical constructions in which he expresses these ideas.

I would not presume to call MacDonald's logic other than straightforward. I think I am on safe ground to say, however, that as his logic progresses it brings in its train multitudinous tangential modifiers and explanations and offshoots that occasionally make it difficult to follow the primary sequence of ideas. Once or twice a page, it seems, I have to stop to read a lengthy section four or five times simply to "get it."

Additionally, MacDonald's grammar and syntax can become extremely involved and can impede understanding. Sentences of one hundred to one hundred twenty words are common, occasionally reaching even two hundred. His paragraphs can run to five or six pages.

For example, the following single sentence from "The Truth," this book's first entry, originally comes to us with one hundred eighty-seven words, thirteen commas, six semicolons, and three dashes:

When the man bows down before a power that can account for him, a power to whom he is no mystery as he is to himself; a power that knows whence he came and whither he is going; who knows why he loves this and hates that, why and where he began to go wrong; who can set him right, longs indeed to set him right, making of him a creature to look up to himself without shadow of doubt, anxiety or fear, confident as a child whom his father is leading by the hand to the heights of happy-making truth, knowing that where he is wrong, the father is right and will set him right; when the man feels his whole being in the embrace of self-responsible paternity—then the man is bursting into his flower; then the truth of his being, the eternal fact at the root of his new name, his real nature, his idea—born in God at first, and responsive to the truth, the being of God, his origin—begins to show itself; then his nature is almost in harmony with itself.

Obviously we understand what MacDonald is expressing. At the same time, with some minor restructuring and re-ordering, his thoughts become more straightforward and accessible. This is especially important when one is attempting to interest new readers in MacDonald's ideas, or when one is encountering him for the first time.

In the first chapter you will find the above quotation not shortened but actually lengthened to two hundred ten words, and restructured into four sentences. This may be a poor example in that one of those four sentences comprises eighty-seven words, and even *that* is usually too long. In other instances I might break up such a single complex sentence into six or eight shorter ones. But it is important that you see what I am seeking to do: The important point is, *nothing has been "left out."* Most of what I have done is more structural than editorial. Clarity, not brevity, has been the goal. I hope to make MacDonald's mind and heart more accessible to us all.

His ideas are here expressed, therefore, in something very close to the manner in which he wrote them. Where his originals are clear and straightforward, they are reproduced without change. Where the word-thickets are complicated and the sentences long, my editing has yet kept most of his actual words intact.

Finally, the subheadings within the text are my own additions. These too are provided as an aid to understanding without materially altering the text.

It seems only fitting, in preparing us at last to move on to the "main course," that we listen once more to Lewis as he describes what made these writings so unique and powerful in his own spiritual development:

> In Macdonald [sic] it is always the voice of conscience that speaks. He addresses the will: the demand for obedience, for "something to be neither more nor less nor other than *done*," is incessant. . . . The Divine Sonship is the key-conception which unites all the different elements of his thought. I dare not say that he is never in error; but to speak plainly I know hardly any other writer who seems to be closer, or more continually close, to the Spirit of Christ himself. Hence his Christlike union of tenderness and severity. Nowhere else outside the New Testament have I found terror and comfort so intertwined. . . . All the sermons are suffused with a spirit of love and wonder. (*George MacDonald, An Anthology*, 18–20)

Michael Phillips
Eureka, California

THE TRUTH

GEORGE MACDONALD

I am the truth.

—JOHN 14:6

When a man of the five senses speaks of *truth*, he regards it as an assertion of something that can be either historically or scientifically proved a fact. If he allows that for anything he knows there may exist yet higher truth, since he cannot obtain proof of it historically or scientifically, he is justified in considering himself under no conceivable obligation to seek other evidence concerning it.

Whatever appeal might be made to the highest region of his nature, the realm of spiritual being, such a one behaves as if the wise man ought to pay such realm no heed because it does not come within the scope of the lower powers of that nature.

According to the word of *the* Man, however, truth means more than fact, more than the relation of facts or persons, more than the loftiest abstraction of spiritual existence.

Rather, it means being and life, will and action. For he says, "I am the truth."

I hope to help those whom I may to understand more of what is meant by *the truth*, not for the sake of definition, or to split logical hairs, but so that when they hear the word from the mouth of the Lord, the right idea will rise in their minds. I desire that the word may neither be a void sound, nor call up either a vague or false notion of what he meant by it. If he says, "I am the truth," it must, to say the least, be well to know what he means by a word so important that he would use it to identify himself.

And immediately we may suppose that he can mean nothing merely intellectual, such as may be set forth and left there. He means something vital—so vital that the whole of its necessary relations are subject to it, so vital that it includes everything else which, in any lower plane, may go or have gone by the same name.

Let us, then, endeavour to arrive at his meaning by a gently ascending stair.

FACT AND TRUTH

If a thing is so, then the word that says it is so is the truth—a true expression of reality. But the fact may be of no value in itself, and our knowledge of it of no value either.

Of most facts it may be said that the truth concerning them is of no consequence. For instance, it cannot be in itself important whether on a certain morning I took one side of the street or the other. It may be of importance to someone to know which I took, but in itself it is of none. It would therefore be unfit if I said, "It is a *truth* that I walked on the sunny side." The correct word would be a *fact*, not a *truth*.

If the question arose whether a statement concerning the thing were correct, we should still be in the region of fact or no fact. But when we come to ask whether the statement was *true* or *false*, then we are concerned with the matter as the assertion of a human being. Immediately we have ascended to another plane of things. It may be of no consequence which side I was on, or it may be of consequence to someone to know which, but it is of *vital* importance to the witness and to any who love him, whether or not he believes the statement he makes—*whether the man himself is true or false.*

Concerning the thing itself it can be but a question of *fact*. It remains a question of fact even whether the man has or has not spoken the truth. But concerning the man himself it is a question of *truth*. He is either a pure soul because he has spoken truly, so far as revealed by this one incident, or a false soul, capable and guilty of a lie. In this relation it is of no consequence whether the man spoke the fact or not. If he meant to speak the fact as he understood it, he remains a true man.

Here I would anticipate so far as to say that there are *truths* as well as *facts*, and lies against truths as well as against facts. When the Pharisees said *corban*, they lied against the truth that a man must honour his father and mother.

FACTS OF LAW

Let us go up now from the region of facts that seem casual to those facts that are invariable and unchangeable—at least we are powerless to change them. These therefore involve what we call *law*.

It will be seen at once that the *fact* here is of more dignity, and the truth or falsehood of a statement in this region of more consequence in itself. It is a small matter whether the water in my jug was frozen on a certain morning. But it is a fact of great importance that at thirty-two degrees Fahrenheit water always freezes. We rise a step here in the nature of the facts concerned.

So I would ask: Have we therefore come into the region of truths? Is it a truth that water freezes at thirty-two degrees?

I think not. There is no principle of truth that we can see that is involved in the changeless fact. The principle that lies at the root of it in the mind of God must be a truth, but to the human mind the fact is as yet only a fact. The word *truth* ought to be kept for higher things.

There are those who think that such facts are the highest that can be known. Therefore they put the highest word they know to the highest thing they know, and call the facts of nature truths. But to me it seems, however high you come in your generalization, however wide you make your law—including, for instance, all solidity under the law of freezing—that you have still not risen higher than the statement that such and such is an invariable fact. Call it a law if you will—a law of nature if you choose. Say that it always is so. But it is not a truth. It cannot be to us a truth until we discern the reason of its existence, its relation to mind and intent, yea to self-existence. Tell us why it *must* be so, and you state a truth.

When we come to see that a law is such because it is the embodiment of a certain eternal thought, beheld by us in it, that it is a fact of the being of God, the facts of which alone are truths, then indeed it will be to us not a law merely, but an embodied truth.

A law of God's nature and essence is a way he would have us think of him. It is a necessary truth of all being. When a law of Nature makes us see this, then we see the truth inherent in the law. When we say, "I understand that law, I see why it ought to be, it is just like God," then that law rises, not merely to the dignity of a truth in itself, but to the truth of its own nature—namely, a revelation of character, nature, and will in God. It is a picture of something in God, a word that tells a fact about God, and is therefore far nearer being called a truth than anything below it.

As a simple illustration: What notion should we have of the unchanging and unchangeable without the solidity of matter? If, such as we are, we had nothing solid about us, how would we be able to think correctly about God and truth and law?

It's as if God were saying,
"I am like this."

WHAT SCIENCE REVEALS OF GOD

But there is a region perhaps not so high as this from the scientific point of view, where yet the word *truth* may begin to be rightly applied.

I believe that every fact in nature is a revelation of God. It exists such as it is because God is such as he is. And I suspect that all its facts impress us so that we learn unconsciously of God.

True, we cannot think of facts in this way unless we find the soul of them—the facts they reveal to us about God. But from the moment we first come into contact with the world, it is to us a revelation of God. The world shows us visible things of his by which we come to know unseen things about him. How should we imagine what we may of God without the firmament over our heads, a visible sphere yet a formless infinitude! What idea could we have of God without the sky? The truth of the sky is what it makes us feel about the very God that placed it before our eyes.

If you say the sky could not but be the way it is, I grant it—with God at the root of it. There is nothing for us to conceive in its place. Therefore, indeed it must be so.

Similarly, in its discovered laws, the waves of light seem to me to be such because God is such. Its so-called laws are the waving of his garments, waving so because he is thinking and loving and walking inside them.

We are here in a region far above that commonly claimed for science. Such revelations are open only to the heart of the child and the childlike man and woman. It is a region in which the poet is among his own things, and a region to which poets often go. For things as they *are*—not merely as science deals with them—are the revelation of God to his children.

I would not be misunderstood. There is no fact of science not yet incorporated in a law, no law of science that has gotten beyond the hypothetical and tentative that does not have the will of God in it. Therefore, all facts and laws of science reveal God. But neither fact nor law is there for the sake of fact or law. Each is but a means to an end. In the perfected end we find the intent, and there we find God—not in the laws themselves except as means to those ends.

For that same reason, human science cannot discover God. Human science is but the backward undoing of the tapestry web of God's science. It works with its back to him, and is always leaving his intent and perfected work behind it. Science is always going farther and farther away from the point where his work culminates in revelation.

Undoubtedly it thus makes some small intellectual approach to him. But at best it can come only to his back. Science will never find the face of God. But those who would reach his heart, those who, like Dante, are returning thither where they are, will find also the springhead of his science.

Analysis is good, as death is good. Analysis is death, not life. It discovers a little of the way God walks to his ends, but in so doing it forgets and leaves the end itself behind. I do not say the man of science does so, but the very process of his work is such a leaving of God's ends behind. It is a tracing back of his footsteps, too often without appreciation of the result for which his feet took those steps.

To rise from the perfected work is the swifter and loftier ascent. If the man could find out *why* God worked so, then he would be discovering God. But even then he would not be discovering the best and the deepest of God. For God's means cannot be so great as his ends.

But I must make myself clearer yet.

THE SCIENTIST, THE POET, AND THE CHILD

Ask a man of mere science what is the truth of a flower. He will pull it to pieces, show you its parts, explain how they operate, how they each contribute to the life of the flower. He will tell you where it grew originally, where it can live, what would be the effects of another climate, and what changes are possible to it through scientific cultivation. He will go on to explain what part the insects have in its variations, and doubtless will tell you many more facts about it.

Ask the poet what is the truth of the flower, and he will answer: "Why, the flower itself, the perfect flower, and what it speaks to him who has ears to hear it."

The *truth* of the flower is not the facts about it, be they correct as ideal science itself can discern them, but the shining, glowing, gladdening, patient thing enthroned on its stalk—the compeller of smiles and tears from child and prophet.

The man of science laughs at this because he is only a man of science. He does not know what it means. But the poet and the child care as little for his laughter as the birds of God, as Dante calls the angels, for his treatise on aerial navigation. The children of God must always be mocked by the children of the world, whether in the church or out of it—children with sharp ears and eyes but dull hearts. Those that hold love as the only good in the world, understand and smile at the world's children, and can do very well without anything they have to tell them. In the higher state to which their love is leading them, they will speedily outstrip the men of science. For they possess that which is at the root of science, that for the revealing of which God's science exists at all.

What shall it profit a man to know all things, and lose the bliss, the consciousness of well-being, which alone can give value to his knowledge?

GOD'S IDEA IN THE FLOWER

God's science in the flower exists for the existence of the flower in its relation to his children. If we understand and are one with, and especially if we love, the flower, we possess that for which the science is there. It is that alone which can equip us for a true search into the ways and means by which the divine idea of the flower was wrought to be presented to us.

The idea of God *is* the flower. His idea is not the botany of the flower. Its botany is but a thing of ways and means—of canvas and colour and brush in relation to the picture in the painter's brain.

The mere intellect can never discover that which owes its being to the heart supreme. The relation of the intellect to that which is born of the heart is unreal except it be a humble one.

The idea of God, I repeat, is the flower. He thought it. He invented its means and sent it as a gift of himself to the eyes and hearts of his children. When we see how they are loved by the ignorant and lowly, we may well believe that flowers have a place in the history of the world—the history written for the archives of heaven which we are yet a long way from understanding. Mere science alone could not, to all eternity, understand this history, nor could the study of it enable anyone to understand it.

Watch that child with the flower! He has found one of his silent and motionless brothers, with God's clothing upon it and God's thought in its face. Behold the smile that breaks out because of the divine understanding between them! Watch his mother when he takes it home to her, though she is no nearer to understanding it than he! It is no old memory that brings those tears to her eyes, powerful in that way as are flowers. Rather, it is God's thought, unrecognized as such, holding communion with her. She weeps with inexplicable delight. Why should she weep—it is only a daisy, only a primrose, only a pheasant's eye narcissus, only a lily of the field, only a snowdrop, only a sweet pea, only a brave yellow crocus! But here to her is no mere fact, no law of nature. Here is a truth of nature, the truth of a flower—a perfect thought from the heart of God—a *truth* of God! It is not an intellectual truth, but a divine fact, a dim revelation, a movement of the creative soul!

Who but a father could think the flowers for his little

ones? And now we are nigh the region in which the Lord's word is at home: "I am the truth."

THE TRUTH OF WATER

Let me offer another illustration that is especially dear to my mind and its special purpose.

What, I ask, is the truth of water? Is it that it is formed of hydrogen and oxygen? That the chemist has such a mode of stating the *fact* of water will not affect my illustration. This explanation of his will probably one day be more antiquated than mine is now. But is it for the sake of the fact that hydrogen and oxygen combine to form water that the precious thing exists? Is pairing oxygen and hydrogen the divine idea of water? Or has God put the two together only that man might separate and find them out?

He allows his child to pull his toys to pieces, but were they made that he might pull them to pieces? He is not a child to be envied for whom his inglorious father would make toys for such an end! A school examiner might see in such experimentation the best use of a toy, but not a father!

Find for us what in the constitution of the two gases makes them fit and capable to be thus honored in forming the lovely thing, and you will give us a revelation about more than water, namely about the God who made oxygen and hydrogen. There is no water in oxygen, no water in hydrogen. It comes bubbling fresh from the imagination of the living God, rushing from under the great white throne of the glacier. The very thought of it makes one gasp with an elemental joy no metaphysician can analyze.

The water itself, that dances and sings and slakes the wonderful thirst—symbol and picture of that thirst for which the woman of Samaria made her prayer to Jesus—this lovely thing itself whose very wetness is a delight to every inch of the human body in its embrace—this live thing which, if I might, I would have running through my room and babbling along my table—this water is its own self, its own truth. Therein it is truth of God.

Let him who would know the love of the maker become sorely thirsty, and drink of the brook at his feet, and then lift up his heart—not at that moment to the maker of oxygen and hydrogen but to the inventor and mediator of thirst and water. Such a man might foresee a little of what his soul may find in God. If he does not then become as a hart panting for the water-brooks, let him go back to his science and its husks. They will at least make him thirsty as the victim in a dust tower of Persia.

As well may a man think to describe the joy of drinking by trying to scientifically analyze thirst and water as imagine that he has revealed anything about water by resolving it into its scientific elements. Let a man go to the hillside and let the brook sing to him till he loves it, and he will find himself far nearer the fountain of truth than the triumphal chariot of the chemist leading the shouting company of his half-comprehending followers. He will draw from the brook the water of joyous tears, and with them worship him that made heaven and earth and sea, and the fountains of waters.

TRUE MANHOOD: DOING TRUTH

We have seen that the moment whatever goes by the name of truth comes into connection with man, everything changes. Instead of merely mirroring itself in his intellect as a thing outside of him, the moment it comes into contact with him as a being of action, the moment the knowledge of that so-called "truth" affects or ought to affect his sense of duty, it becomes a thing of far nobler import. The question of truth then enters upon a higher phase and looks out a loftier window. A fact which in itself is of no value becomes at once a matter of life and death—moral life and death—when a man has the imperative choice of being true or false concerning it.

When the truth, the heart, the summit, the crown of a thing, is perceived by a man, he approaches the fountain of truth whence the thing came. Perceiving God by a right understanding of what exists in the world around him, he becomes more of a man, more of the being he was meant to be. In virtue of this perceived truth, he now enters into relations with the universe which were undeveloped in him till then.

But far higher even than this will the *doing* of the most insignificant duty raise him. It is then that he begins thereby to be a true man.

A man may delight in the vision and glory of a truth, and not himself be true. The man whose vision is weak, but who, as far as he sees, and desirous to see further, *does* the thing he sees, is a true man. If a man knows what is, and says it is not, his knowing does not make him less than a liar. The man who recognizes the truth of any human relation, and neglects the duty involved, is not a true man. The man who knows the laws of nature and does not heed them, the more he teaches them to others the less is he a true man. But he may obey them all and be the falsest of men because of far higher and closer duties which he neglects. The man who takes good care of himself and none of his brother and sister is false.

A poet may be aware of the highest truth of a thing and of that beauty which is the final cause of its existence. He may draw from that beauty a sense of the creative loveliness that thought it out. He may be a man who would not tell a lie or steal or slander. Yet with all this he may not yet be a true man inasmuch as the essentials of manhood are not his life's goal. He has not come to the flower of his own higher being or attained the truth for which he exists—the idea of his being for which he was created. Neither is he even striving toward it. There are relations closer than those of the facts around him, plainer than those that seem to bring the maker nigh to him, which he is failing to see. Or, if he does see, he fails to acknowledge and fulfill them.

Man is man only in the *doing* of the truth, perfect man only in the doing of the highest truth, which is the fulfilling of his relations to his origin.

DUTY: THE DOING OF TRUTH
TOWARD THOSE AROUND US

But he has relations with his fellowman, closer infinitely than with any of the things around him, and to many a man far plainer than his relations with God. And God has made the nearer more plain to our understandings in order that we may fulfill it, and thus rise to the higher which is less understandable. Our relations with those around us make a large part of our being. They are essential to our very existence and spring from the very facts of the origination of our beings.

They are the relation of thought to thought, of being to being, of duty to duty. The very nature of a man depends upon or is one with these relations. They are *truths*, and the man is a true man as he fulfils them. Fulfilling them perfectly, he is himself a *truth*, a living truth.

As regarded merely by the intellect, these human relationships are facts of man's nature. But that they are of man's *nature* makes them truths, and the fulfillments of them are duties. Man is so constituted as to understand his relations with his fellows at first more than he can love them. And this has the resulting advantage of giving him the opportunity to choose the duties associated with them purely because they are true. So doing, he chooses to love them, and is enabled to love them in the doing, which alone can truly reveal them more deeply to him and make the loving of them possible. Then they cease to show themselves in the form of duties at all and appear as they more truly are—absolute truths, essential realities, eternal delights.

The man is a true man who chooses duty. He is a perfect man who at length never thinks of duty and forgets the very name of it. The duty of Jesus was the doing in lower than perfect forms that which he loved perfectly and did perfectly in the highest forms also. Thus he fulfilled all righteousness.

Relations, truths, duties, are shown to the man far beyond him that he may choose them and be a child of God—choosing righteousness like him. Hence the whole sad, victorious human tale, and the glory to be revealed!

The moral philosopher who regards duties only as facts of his system, and even the man who regards them as essential realities of his humanity but goes no further, is essentially a liar—a man of untruth. He is a man indeed, but not a true man. He is a man in possibility, but not a real man yet.

The recognition of these things brings with it the imperative obligation to fulfill them. Not fulfilling these relations, the man is undoing the right of his own existence and destroying his *raison d'être*. He is making of himself a live reason why he should not continue living, for nothing could ever have begun to be that refused to fulfill its reason for being.

The facts of human relation, then, are truths indeed of hugest import. "Whosoever hateth his brother is a murderer; and ye know that no murderer hath eternal life abiding in him!" The man who lives as a hunter after pleasure, not a labourer in the fields of duty, who thinks of himself as if he were alone on the earth, is in himself a lie. Instead of being the man he was made to be, he lives as the beasts seem to live. There is, however, this difference. I trust that they are rising while he, in what he is making of himself, is sinking.

But he cannot be allowed to sink beyond God's reach. Hence, all the holy—that is, healing—miseries that come upon him, of which he complains as so hard and unfair, exist for the compelling of the truth to which he will not yield.

They represent a painful persuasion calling him to be himself and thus be a truth.

LONGING FOR THE HIGHEST OF ALL RELATIONS

But suppose, for the sake of my progressive unfolding, that a man did everything required of him—fulfilled all the relations to his fellows of which I have been speaking, and was, toward them at least, a true man. He would still feel that something was lacking in him. Indeed, such a one would undoubtedly feel it all the more. He would feel that something was lacking to his necessary well-being. Like a live flower, he would feel that he had not yet blossomed, and could not tell what the blossom ought to be.

The words of the Lord point in this direction when he says to the youth, "If thou wouldst be perfect." Such a man would feel that his existence was not yet justified to itself, that the truth of his being and nature was not yet fully revealed to his consciousness. He would remain unsatisfied. And the cause would be that there was in him a hunger for a relation which had not yet come into live fact, which had not yet become a truth in him. The deepest, closest, and strongest of all relations possible had not ripened into the divine idea which alone can content itself with its being.

A child with a child's heart who does not even know that he has a father, yet longs for him with his whole nature, even if not with his consciousness. This relation has not yet so far begun to be fulfilled in him. The coming blossom sends before it patience and hope enough to enable him to live by faith without sight. When the flower begins to come, the human plant begins to rejoice in the glory of God not yet revealed, the inheritance of the saints in light. With uplifted stem and forward-leaning bud, it expects the hour when the lily of God's field shall know itself alive, with God himself for its heart and its air. In its deepest being it anticipates the hour when God and man shall be one, and all that God cares for shall be man's. But again I get ahead of my progression.

EXERCISING THE WILL IN HARMONY WITH OUR ORIGIN

The highest truth to the intellect, the abstract truth, is the relation in which man stands to the source of his being. It is the relationship of his will to the Will through which it became a will, the relationship of his love to the Love that kindled his power to love, the relationship of his intellect to the Intellect that lighted his.

If a man deal with these things only as objects of thought, as ideas to be analyzed and arranged in their due order and right relation, he treats them as facts and not as truths. He is no better—and probably much the worse—for his analytical thought about them, for his knowledge is incomplete and he is false to all that is most worthy of his faithfulness.

But when the soul, or heart, or spirit, or whatever you please to call that which is the man himself and not his body, becomes aware that he needs some One above him whom to obey, in whom to rest, from whom to seek deliverance from what in himself is despicable, disappointing, and unworthy, then indeed is that man approaching the region of truth. When he is aware of an opposition in him which is not in harmony, when he recognizes that there is present within him, seeming to be himself—what sometimes is called *the old Adam*, sometimes *the flesh*—a lower nature that is his evil self and is a part of his being where God is not, then he is beginning to come true in himself.

And it will not be long before he discovers that there is no part in him with which he would be at strife if God were there. That part of him would be true, what it ought to be, and in right relation to the whole. For by whatever name you call it, the old Adam, or an unruly horse or dog or tiger, with God at home within him it would then fulfill its holy function, intruding upon nothing, subject utterly to the rule of the higher. Horse or dog or tiger or Adam, it would be a good horse, good dog, good tiger, good man.

When the man bows down before a power that can account for him, a power to whom he is no mystery as he is to himself, then the man is bursting into his flower. When he acknowledges the power that knows whence he came and whither he is going, who knows why he loves this and hates that, who knows why and where he began to go wrong, and who can set him right and indeed longs to set him right, then the truth of his being, the eternal fact at the root of his new name, has begun to show itself. When he kneels before the God whose desire is to make of him a creature able to look up to himself without shadow of doubt or anxiety or fear, confident as a child whom his father is leading by the hand to the heights of happy-making truth, knowing that where he is wrong, the father is right and will set him right, then his real nature—an idea born in God at first, and newly responsive to the truth of his origin—has begun to come alive. When the man feels his whole being in the embrace of self-responsible fatherhood, then his nature is in harmony with itself.

Obeying the will that is the cause of his being, the cause of that which demands of itself to be true—that will being righteousness and love and truth—he begins to stand on the apex of his being. He begins to know his divine origins. He begins to feel himself free.

The truth has made him free. This is not trueness known merely to his intellect, but truth as revealed in his own sense of being true, truth known by his essential consciousness of his divine condition. Without such truth, his nature is neither his own nor God's.

Not any abstract truth, not all abstract truth, not the purest spiritual insight toward any spiritual truth, can make any man free. The truth done, the truth loved, the truth lived . . . the truth *of* and not merely *in* the man . . . the honesty that makes him a child of the honest God—only such truth can make him free.

BECOMING A LIVE TRUTH: CHRIST IN US

When with his whole nature, a man is loving and willing the truth, he is then a live truth. But this he has not originated in himself. He has seen it and striven for it, but not originated it. The one originating, living, visible truth, embracing all truths in all relations, is Jesus Christ. He is true. He is the live Truth. His truth, chosen and willed by him, the ripeness of his being, the flower of the sonship which is his nature, the crown of his topmost perfect relation acknowledged and gloried in, is his absolute obedience to his Father.

The obedient Jesus is Jesus the Truth. He is true and is the root of all truth and development of truth in men. Their very being, however far from the true human, is the undeveloped Christ in them. His likeness to Christ is the truth of a man, in the same way that the perfect meaning of a flower is the truth of a flower.

Every man, according to the divine idea of him, must enter into the truth of that idea. The truth of every man is the perfected Christ in him. As Christ is the blossom of humanity, so the blossom of every man is the Christ perfected in him.

The vital force of humanity working in him is Christ. He is his root—the generator and perfecter of his individuality. The stronger the pure will of the man to be true, the freer and more active his choice, the more definite his individuality, ever the more is the man and all that is his, Christ's.

Without him we could not have been. Being, we could not have become capable of truth. Capable of truth, we could never have loved it. Loving and desiring it, we could not have attained to it.

Nothing but the heart-presence, the humanest sympathy, and whatever other deeper thing may be between the creating

Truth and the responding soul, could make a man go on hop-
ing, until at last he forges himself, and begins keeping an open
house for God to come and go. He gives us the will wherewith to will and the power to use it. He gives the help
needed—whatever that need may in any case be—to supple-
ment the power. But we ourselves must *will* the truth. And
for that the Lord is waiting, for that victory of God his Father
in the heart of his child. In this alone can the travail of his
own soul be satisfied. The work is his, but we must take our
willing share.

When the blossom breaks forth in us, the more it is ours
the more it is his. For the highest creation of the Father, and
that preeminently through the Son, is the being that can, like
the Father and the Son, of his own self will what is right. The
groaning and travailing, the blossom and the joy, are the
Father's and the Son's and ours. The will—the power of willing—may be created, but the willing itself is begotten.
Because God wills first, man wills also.

When my being is consciously and willfully in the hands
of him who called it to live and think and suffer and be glad—
given back to him by a perfect obedience—I thenceforward
breathe the breath and share the life of God himself. Then I
am free, in that I am true—which means one with the Father.
And freedom knows itself to be freedom.

When a man is true, even if he were in hell he could not
be miserable. He is right with himself because he is right with
him from whom he came. To be right with God is to be right
with the universe. It is to be one with the power, the love,
the will of the mighty Father, the cherisher of joy, the lord of

laughter, whose are all glories, all hopes, who loves everything, and hates nothing but selfishness, which he will not have in his kingdom.

Christ then is the Lord of life. His life is the light of men. The light mirrored in them changes them into the image of him, *Jesus the Truth.*

Insights Into

THE TRUTH

MICHAEL PHILLIPS

During his lifetime, George MacDonald penned eight nonfiction books of essays and sermons that established him as a theologian and Christian thinker and apologist of significance in his time. In our own day, however, it is mostly as a writer of compelling fiction that he is well known and remembered. There are many avid MacDonald readers who do not realize the singular impact he has had on Christian theology and its perception of God's character and work.

This series of books, arranged topically from MacDonald's essays and sermons, provides the spiritual foundation upon which MacDonald's thirty-five or forty fiction works are built.

MacDonald the Scientist

The selection you have just read, "The Truth," from George MacDonald's original book entitled *Unspoken Sermons, Third Series*, is one of my own favorite MacDonald sermons/essays. In it he skillfully weaves threads of poet, scientist, and theologian together into a wonderfully insightful tapestry that reveals more "truth" about Truth than nearly anything I have ever read.

MacDonald was a man of multiple dimensions, which accounts for the breadth and depth of his writing. He was no mere novelist—he was a poet of renown, a preacher who was once offered one of America's most prestigious pulpits, a theologian who is still influencing Christian thought, a historian, a student of Shakespeare, an editor, and an author of numerous children's stories and fairy tales and fantasies.

But in all this, what many do not realize is that MacDonald was also a scientist. Before entering theological school to work toward his divinity degree in hopes of a career in the church, MacDonald's major fields of undergraduate studies were in chemistry and natural philosophy, or what is now called physics. What a surprising educational background for a man who became such a literary giant and an imaginative theological influence. Truly must both the analytical and creative halves of his brain have functioned in perfect harmony and at peak capacity!

And in what an era for science he participated! MacDonald lived through a scientific revolution throughout the latter half of the nineteenth century, from Darwin's work to the major developments in biology, chemistry, electromagnetism, radiation, medicine, and dozens of other fields. The industrial revolution reached its zenith, the internal combustion engine was invented . . . electricity . . . the telephone . . . it was an era of explosive growth and change. If one were to list the top ten discoveries in every scientific discipline, probably half or more from each list would come from during MacDonald's lifetime. He was a contemporary of many who are still considered the greatest names in science.

Surely all these inventions and developments fascinated him. It is probable that he subscribed to scientific journals and kept pace with discoveries in many fields. I think there is little doubt he could have enjoyed a successful career in either chemistry or physics. Just imagine his creative and inventive mind focused on the scientific dilemmas of the day! What might George MacDonald have contributed to the scientific discussion had he been working alongside Darwin or one of the great physicists of the day?

How grateful we of his spiritual posterity are that he pursued these "first loves" no more than he did his "second love" of the professional clergy, and instead made his pen the chosen instrument of his trade rather than the test tube, the microscope, or the pulpit. Indeed, MacDonald's pen turned out to be a *spiritual* telescope through which he explored the reaches of God's character that lay beyond the vision of mortal man, as well as a far-reaching *pulpit* from which his voice is still reaching millions across a century of time. Such is the purpose of this series of books, to sharpen with the aid of a new lens those spiritual queries and questions MacDonald's great heart explored, so that we might look through his spiritual telescope with greater clarity of vision.

In "The Truth," MacDonald draws upon his scientific background to distinguish between *fact, law,* and *truth.* As he does, he speaks often of "the man of science." The phrase is amusing given that he himself was such a one. Had he already, during his undergraduate years at Kings College in Aberdeen, in the early 1840s, as much as he loved raw science for itself, begun to recognize the limitations of what life-revelations that science was capable of providing? Were such realizations part of his own eventual decision to give himself to another branch of investigation and inquiry that took up where science left off?

MacDonald did not directly chronicle his own spiritual story. We are left to speculate how this transition of focus and emphasis took place in his mind and heart. For the most part, the only insights we have into the development of his perspectives come from his writings. We are, however, given additional glimpses of science's pull on his young and expanding brain in the essay "A Sketch of Individual Development," found in one of his lesser known books, oddly entitled *Orts.*

MacDonald's Ascending Stair

With this background, then, let us see what renaissance man George MacDonald (poet and scientist, theologian and novelist, historian and allegorist, translator and editor, preacher and father) has to tell us about *truth.*

After laying his foundation in the word of Jesus that *he* is "the truth," MacDonald embarks upon a progression of thought he calls "a gently ascending stair." The first step upon this stair is the distinction between fact and truth. In so distinguishing, he establishes the theme he will develop in increasing depth as he goes along—that truth must concern *individuals* rather than raw scientific *facts*. It is upon the basis of how men and women respond to facts—as living and breathing *people*, moral agents with wills of their own—that truth is established. Facts cannot in themselves be truths. It is a man's *response* to facts that can either be true or false.

> If a thing is so, then the word that says it is so is the truth—a true expression of reality. But the fact may be of no value in itself. . . .
>
> If the question arose whether a statement concerning the thing were correct, we should still be in the region of fact or no fact. But when we come to ask whether the statement was *true* or *false*, then we are concerned with the matter as the assertion of a human being. Immediately we have ascended to another plane of things. . . .
>
> Concerning the thing itself it can be but a question of *fact*. . . . But concerning the man himself it is a question of *truth*.

On the basis of unchangeable scientific facts, laws are established. MacDonald says that "we rise a step here in the nature of the facts concerned." But we are still not in the region of truth, no matter how wide we make our law. "The word *truth*," he adds, "ought to be kept for higher things."

Truth, he says, must probe the region of *why*, the region of *will*, the region of God's intent and being.

When we say, "I understand that law, I see why it ought to be, it is just like God," then that law rises, not merely to the dignity of a truth in itself, but to the truth of its own nature—namely, a revelation of character, nature, and will in God. It is a picture of something in God, a word that tells a fact about God, and is therefore far nearer being called a truth than anything below it.

SCIENCE: A REVELATION OF GOD

Perhaps it is only a scientist who can place science in its proper perspective. So much of the nineteenth-century debate and controversy between "science" and "religion" (as, indeed, also in our own time), given great impetus by Darwin but extending far beyond evolutionary theory, was wrongly directed toward an either/or argument. If *science* was to be the new basis for understanding the truth of the universe (said the scientists), then God and faith had no more contribution to make. They could be relegated to the scrap heap of outdated historical notions. If *God and faith*, on the other hand, remained the basis for truth (said Christians), then science was untrustworthy, unreliable, and anti-God in its bias and focus.

This either/or fallacy, pitting science and faith *against* each other, was, and remains, a false debate. Those who engage in it (and naturalists and Christians remain hotly embroiled in it a century later) are mistaken on both sides. They understand neither science nor faith and the fundamental role both play in the fulfillment and complete understanding of the other.

It took MacDonald, a scientist of faith, to place *both* in harmony and perspective. Faith is not threatened by science. Nor can science explain root causes and high meanings. They work *together*, not in different arenas of inquiry but from distinct vantage points within the *same* arena—namely, the universe—to point us toward truth . . . and ultimately to reveal, each contributing its own unique perspective to that revelation, the Creator of that universe.

> Every fact in nature is a revelation of God. It exists such as it is because God is such as he is. . . . The world shows us visible things of his by which we come to know unseen things about him. . . .
>
> There is no fact of science . . . that does not have the will of God in it. Therefore, all facts and laws of science reveal God. But . . . human science cannot discover God. Human science is but the backward undoing of the tapestry-web of God's science. It works with its back to him, and is always leaving his intent and perfected work behind it. Science is always going farther and farther away from the point where his work culminates in revelation . . . at best it can come only to his back. Science will never find the face of God. . . . It is a tracing back of his footsteps, too often without appreciation of the result for which his feet took those steps.

THE TRUTH OF FLOWERS AND WATER

To balance what MacDonald calls "the man of science," he now brings the poet and the child (both of which—the former literally, the latter spiritually—are also self-portraits of MacDonald himself) into his ascending discussion. Their distinctive responses to nature—in this case, a flower—along with that of the scientist, give us three windows (all three originating within his own heart and brain) into the revelation that what we call *truth* can only be discovered by making closer approach to the *meaning* God intends the things of his creation to possess.

God's science in the flower exists for the existence of the flower in its relation to his children. If we understand and are one with, and especially if we love the flower, we possess that for which the science is there. It is that alone which can equip us for a true search into the means and ways by which the divine idea of the flower was wrought out to be presented to us.

The idea of God *is* the flower. . . . He thought it. He invented its means and sent it as a gift of himself to the eyes and hearts of his children. . . .

Who but a father could think the flowers for his little ones? And now we are nigh the region in which the Lord's word is at home—"I am the truth."

From flowers, MacDonald makes the same point using water as his illustration:

What, I ask, is the truth of water? Is it that it is formed of hydrogen and oxygen? . . . Or has God put the two together only that man might separate and find them out? . . .

Find for us what in the constitution of the two gases makes them fit and capable to be thus honoured in forming the lovely thing, and you will give us a revelation about more than water, namely about the God who made oxygen and hydrogen. There is no water in oxygen, no water in hydrogen. It comes bubbling fresh from the imagination of the living God, rushing from under the great white throne of the glacier. . . . This water is its own self, its own truth. Therein it is truth of God.

Let him who would know the love of the maker become sorely thirsty, and drink of the brook at his feet, and then lift up his heart—not at that moment to the maker of oxygen and hydrogen but to the inventor and mediator of thirst and water. Such a man might foresee a little of what his soul may find in God.

THE TRUTH OF MAN

With these foundations, MacDonald returns to where he began—to inquire of truth in relation to man. Having progressed up his "gently ascending stair" of understanding, however, he raises the discussion to an altogether higher plane. He now marries the knowing and perceiving of truth with the duty inherent in that knowing. The *doing* of truth— even the doing of partial truth, if it is all one is capable of at the time—thus becomes the doorway into being a "true" man or woman.

> Man is man only in the *doing* of the truth, perfect man only in the doing of the highest truth, which is the fulfilling of his relations to his origin.

MacDonald identifies two chief regions of "duty" incumbent upon man which, to fulfill, makes us true men: Duty toward men, and duty toward God.

Even the unbelieving world, fulfilling it however imperfectly, has little difficulty recognizing man's moral obligations toward his fellowmen. Far less, however, does it acknowledge man's relation to God, the source of his life, as the causative foundation of ultimate truth. But, MacDonald maintains, there is no completeness of truth apart from our origin. Men can *talk* of truth, but to know truth in any complete sense requires a personal response to his origin.

> When the soul, or heart, or spirit . . . becomes aware that he needs some One above him whom to obey . . . then indeed is that man approaching the region of truth. . . .
>
> When the man bows down before a power that can account for him . . . then the man is bursting into his flower. When he acknowledges the power that knows whence he came and whither he is going . . . then the truth of his being . . . has begun to show itself. When he kneels before the God whose desire is to make of him a creature able to look up to himself without shadow of doubt or anxiety or fear . . . then his real nature . . . has

begun to come alive. When the man feels his whole being in the embrace of self-responsible fatherhood, then his nature is in harmony with itself. . . .

The truth has made him free. This is not trueness known merely to his intellect, but truth as revealed in his own sense of being true. (See chart, p. 49.)

LIVE TRUTH: BLOSSOM OF THE HUMAN FLOWER

· At last MacDonald ascends to his climax.

The required personal response to our origin is fulfilled in our personal response to the Man who came from that originating Source and was himself one with it. There is little more to be said, for MacDonald has said it:

> The one originating, living, visible truth, embracing all truths in all relations, is Jesus Christ. He is true. He is the live Truth . . . the root of all truth and development of truth in men. . . .
>
> Every man, according to the divine idea of him, must enter into the truth of that idea. The truth of every man is the perfected Christ in him. As Christ is the blossom of humanity, so the blossom of every man is the Christ perfected in him. . . .
>
> Without him we could not have been. Being, we could not have become capable of truth. Capable of truth, we could never have loved it. Loving and desiring it, we could not have attained to it. . . . He gives us the will wherewith to will, and the power to use it. . . . But we ourselves must *will* the truth. . . . The work is his, but we must take our willing share. . . .

For the highest creation of the Father, and that preeminently through the Son, is the being that can, like the Father and the Son, of his own self will what is right. . . .

When my being is consciously and willfully in the hands of him who called it to live and think and suffer and be glad—given back to him by a perfect obedience—I thenceforward breathe the breath and share the life of God himself.

Creation	Man	God

Scientific facts

↓

Scientific law ────────────────────────→ What does God mean by
the facts and laws of science?

↓

Revelation of God's
being through creation

Man's response to
facts and events
(true or false)

The "truth" of science
(God's intent, what it
reveals of God's nature)

Jesus Christ—
God's revealed truth in humanity:
(The perfect man)

The "truth" of man
(Becoming what
God intends)

The perfection of man—
Truth fulfilled
(Christ in man)

THE TRUTH IN JESUS

GEORGE MACDONALD

But ye did not so learn Christ; if so be that ye heard him,
and were taught in him, even as truth, is in Jesus: that ye
put away, as concerning your former manner of life, the old
man, which waxeth corrupt after the lusts of deceit.[1]
—EPHESIANS 4:20–22

HAVE WE LEARNED JESUS HIMSELF OR ONLY ABOUT HIM?

How have we learned Christ? It ought to be a startling thought that we may have learned him wrong.

---

[1]That is, "which is still going to ruin through the love of the lie."

That is a far worse thing than not to have learned him at all, for his place in our minds is occupied by a false Christ that is hard to exorcize. The point is whether we have learned Christ as he taught himself, or as *men* who thought they understood but did not understand him, have taught us about him. Do we only think we know him—with fleshly notions that come from low, mean human fancies and explanations? Or do we truly know him—after the spirit, in our limited measure, in the same way as God knows him?

Throughout its history, the Christian faith has been open to more corrupt misrepresentation than the Jewish could ever be. As it is higher and wider, so must it yield larger scope to corruption. Have we learned of Christ in false statements and corrupted lessons about him, or have we learned *himself*? Nay, true or false, is our brain only full of things concerning him, or does he dwell himself in our hearts, a learnt, and ever being learnt lesson, the power of our life?

I have been led to what I am about to say by a certain statement made by one who is in the front rank of those who assert that man can know and ascertain nothing about the existence of an infinite higher Power from whom all things proceed. His statement is this:

> The visiting on Adam's descendants through hundreds of generations dreadful penalties for a small transgression which they did not commit; the damning of all men who do not avail themselves of an alleged mode of obtaining forgiveness, which most men have never heard of; and the effecting a reconciliation by sacrificing a son who was perfectly innocent, to satisfy the assumed necessity for a pro-

pitiatory victim; are modes of action which, ascribed to a human ruler, would call forth expressions of abhorrence; and the ascription of them to the Ultimate Cause of things, even now felt to be full of difficulties, must become impossible.

I do not quote the passage with the design of opposing it, for I entirely agree with it. Indeed, it almost feels an absurdity to say so. Neither do I propose addressing a word to its writer or to any who agree with his belief in man's incapacity to know God. My purpose here is altogether differently directed.

One of my earliest recollections is of beginning to be at strife with the false system here assailed. Such paganism I scorn as heartily in the name of Christ as I scorn it in the name of righteousness. Rather than believe a single point involving its spirit, even with the assurance thereby of such salvation as the system offers, I would join the ranks of those who "know nothing," and set myself with hopeless heart to what I am now trying with an infinite hope in the help of the pure originating One—to get rid of my miserable mean self, comforted only by the chance that death would either leave me with no more thought, or else might reveal something of the Ultimate Cause which it would not be an insult to him, or a dishonor to his creature, to hold concerning him. Even such a chance alone might enable one to live.

WHY DO MEN NOT INQUIRE MORE DEEPLY INTO MATTERS OF BELIEF?

I will not now inquire how it comes that the writer of the passage quoted seems to put forward these so-called beliefs as representing Christianity. Nor will I ask why he would think such a creed representative of those who call themselves Christians, seeing that many—some of them of higher rank in literature than himself—believe in Christ with true hearts, and hold to not one of such things as he has set down. He would doubtless be surprised at how many sincere Christians hold them in at least as great abhorrence as he.

His answer would probably be that, even had he been aware of such fact that his statement was not an accurate reflection of the beliefs of *all* Christians, what he had been trying to deal with was the forming and ruling notions of religious society. He would insist that such *are* the views held by the bulk of both educated and uneducated calling themselves Christians, even though some of them may vainly think by an explanatory clause here and there to lessen the disgracefulness of their falsehood. And sadly, that such are the things so held, I am, alas! unable to deny.

It helps nothing, I repeat, that some—thinking seriously very little on the matter—use *quasi* mitigated forms to express their doctrines, and imagine that they indicate a different class of ideas. It would require but a brief examination to be convinced that they are not merely analogous—they are ultimately identical.

But were I to address the writer, I should ask why he had not examined the matter in greater depth. Why is it that, refusing these dogmas as abominable and in themselves plainly false, yet knowing that they are attributed to men whose Christian teaching has done more to civilize the world than that of any other belief or religion, and if such ideas as he represents could not have done so—why has he not taken such pains of enquiry as must surely have satisfied a man of his intelligence that they were *not* the teaching of such men? I would ask him to consider whether the reason for this may not lie in the fact that their beliefs were actually so *different,* and so *good,* that even the forced companionship of such horrible lies as those he has recounted has been unable to destroy their regenerative power throughout history.

I suppose he will allow that there was a man named Jesus who died for the truth he taught. Can he believe that he died for such alleged truth as he has set down? Would it not be well, I would ask him, to inquire what he did *really* teach, according to the primary sources of our knowledge of him?

If he answered that the question was uninteresting to him, I should have no more to say. Nor did I now start to speak of him except with the object of making my position plain to those to whom I would speak—not unbelievers such as himself, but those, namely, who *do* call themselves Christians.

If I should ask those, as I said, who call themselves Christians, "How has it come about that such opinions as the above writer has set down are actually held concerning the Holy One, whose ways you take upon you to set forth?" most of them would answer, "Those are the things he tells us himself in his Word. We have learned them from the Scriptures."

Many also would set forth explanations which appear to

explain the things in such a way that makes them no longer seem so villainous. Still others would remark that better ideas, though largely held by individuals within Christendom, had not yet had time to show themselves as the belief of the religious leaders and thinkers of the nation.

WHAT ARE WE CONVEYING TO OUR GENERATION: OPINION OR TRUTH?

Of those whose presentation of Christian doctrine is represented in the quotation above, there are two classes— those who are *content* it should be so, and those to whom such doctrines are *grievous* but who do not see how to get rid of them.

To the latter it may be some little comfort to have one who has studied the New Testament for many years, and loves it beyond the power of speech can express, declare to them his conviction that there is not an atom of such teaching in the whole lovely, divine utterance. I declare further that such an explanation of essential Christian doctrine is all and altogether the invention of men—honest invention, in part at least, I grant, but still false.

Thank God, we are not bound to accept any man's explanation of God's ways and God's doings, however good the man may be, if it does not commend itself to our conscience. The man's conscience may be a better conscience than ours, and his judgment clearer. Yet still we cannot accept that which we cannot see to be good. To do so would be to sin.

But it is by no means my object to set forth what I believe or do not believe. A time may come for that. My design is now very different indeed. I desire to address those who call themselves Christians and expostulate with them thus:

Whatever be your *opinions* on the greatest of all subjects, is it well that the impression with regard to Christianity made upon your generation should be that of mere opinion, or should it not come from something beyond opinion?

Is Christianity even capable of being represented by *opinion*, even the best of opinion? If it were, how many of us are such as God would choose to represent his thoughts and intents by *our* opinions concerning them? Who is there of his friends whom any thoughtful man would depute to represent his thoughts to his fellows?

If you answer, "The opinions I hold and by which I represent Christianity are those of the Bible," I reply that none can understand, still less represent, the opinions of another, but such as are of the same mind with him. Certainly no one who *mistakes* his whole scope and intent, so far as in supposing *opinion* to be the object of any writer in the Bible, could be capable of accurately representing such a writer.

Is Christianity a system of articles of belief, even if they are correct as language can give them? Never.

I am so far from believing it that I would rather that a man held, as numbers of you do, what seem to me the most obnoxious untruths, opinions the most irreverent and gross, if at the same time he *lived* in the faith of the Son of God— that is, trusted in God as the Son of God trusted in him—

than I would have a man hold formulas of belief that co-
incided at every point with my own if he knew nothing of a
daily life and walk with God. The one, holding doctrines of
devils, is yet a child of God. The other, holding the doctrines of Christ and his apostles, is of the world, yea, of the
devil.

What! A man hold the doctrine of devils and yet be of
God?

Yes—for to hold a thing with the intellect is not to
believe it. A man's real belief is that which he lives by. And
if a man lives by the love of God and obedience to his law
so far as he has recognized it, even if he holds, as I say, to
certain hideous doctrines, those false beliefs are actually
outside of him. He *thinks* they are inside, but no matter.
They are not true and cannot really be inside any good man.
They are sadly against him, for he cannot love to dwell upon
any of those supposed characteristics of his God. He acts
and lives nevertheless in a measure like the true God.

What a man believes is the thing he *does*. Many a good
man would shrink with loathing from actions such as his
doctrine justifies God in doing. Like God, he loves and helps
and saves. Will the living God let such a man's opinions
damn him? No more than he will let the correct opinions of
another, who lives for himself, save him. The best salvation
even the latter could give would be but damnation.

What I come to and insist upon is that, supposing your
theories right, even suppose they contain all that is to be
believed, yet those theories are not what makes you Christians, if Christians indeed you are. On the contrary, they

are, with not a few of you, just what *keeps* you from being Christians.

PLANS OF SALVATION OFFER NO SALVATION

When you say that to be saved a man must hold this or that, then you are forsaking the living God and his will and putting trust in some notion *about* him or his will. To make my meaning clearer: Some of you say that we must trust in the finished work of Christ. Or you say that our faith must be in the merits of Christ—in the atonement he has made—in the blood he has shed.

All these statements are a simple repudiation of the living Lord *in whom* we are told to believe. It is his presence with and in us, and our obedience to him, that lifts us out of darkness into light and leads us from the kingdom of Satan into the glorious liberty of the sons of God. No manner or amount of belief *about him* is the faith of the New Testament.

With such teaching I have had a lifelong acquaintance, and I declare it most miserably false. But I do not now mean to dispute against it. Except the light of the knowledge of the glory of God in the face of Christ Jesus make a man sick of his opinions, he may hold them to doomsday as far as I am concerned.

No opinion, I repeat, is Christianity, and no preaching of any plan of salvation is the preaching of the glorious gospel of the living God. Even if your plan, your theories, were absolutely true, the holding of them with sincerity, the trusting in

this or that about Christ, or in anything he did or could do—
the trusting in anything but himself, his own living self—is
still a delusion.

Many will grant this heartily. And yet the moment you
come to talk with them, you find they insist that to believe in
Christ is to believe in the atonement, meaning by that only
and altogether their special theory about the atonement. And
when you say we must believe in the atoning Christ, and cannot possibly believe in any *theory* concerning the atonement,
they go away and denounce you, saying, "He does not believe
in the atonement!"

If I explain the atonement otherwise than they explain it,
they assert that I deny the atonement, and count it of no consequence that I say I believe in the atoner with my whole
heart, and soul, and strength, and mind. This they call *con-
tending for the truth!*

Because I refuse an explanation that is not in the New
Testament, though they believe it *is* because they can think of
no other—an explanation which seems to me as false in logic
as detestable in morals, not to say that there is no spirituality
in it whatever—therefore they say I am not a Christian!

Small wonder that men such as I quoted at the beginning
refuse the Christianity they suppose such "believers" to represent!

I do not say that this sad folly may not mingle with it a
potent faith in the Lord himself. But I do say that the importance they place on theory is even more sadly obstructive to
true faith than such theories themselves. While the mind is
occupied in enquiring, "Do I believe or feel this thing right?"

the true question is forgotten: "Have I left all to follow him?"

To the man who gives himself to the living Lord, every belief will necessarily come right. The Lord himself will see that his disciple believe aright concerning him. If a man cannot trust him for this, what claim can he make to faith in him? It is because he has little or no faith that he is left clinging to preposterous and dishonouring ideas, holding onto the traditions of men concerning his Father rather than his own teaching or that of his apostles.

The living Christ is to them but a shadow. No soul can thoroughly believe in the all-but-obliterated Christ of their theories. The disciple of such a Christ rests on his work, or his merits, or his atonement!

FAITH IN CHRIST: DOING WHAT HE SAID

What I insist upon is that a man's faith shall be in the living, loving, ruling, helping Christ, devoted to us as much as he ever was, and devoted with all the powers of the Godhead to the salvation of his brethren. It is not faith that he did this, or that his work wrought that—it is faith in the man who did and is doing everything for us that will save him. Without this he cannot work to heal spiritually, any more than he would heal physically when he was present to the eyes of men.

Do you ask, "What is faith in him?"

I answer, the leaving of your way, your objects, your self, and the taking of his and him. It is the leaving of your trust in men, in money, in opinion, in character, in atonement itself, *and doing as he tells you.*

I can find no words strong enough to serve for the weight of this necessity—this obedience. It is the one terrible heresy of the church that it has always been presenting something else than obedience as faith in Christ. The work of Christ is not the working Christ, any more than the clothing of Christ is the body of Christ. If the woman who touched the hem of his garment had trusted in the garment and not in him who wore it, would she have been healed? The reason that so many who believe *about* Christ rather than in him get the comfort they do, is that touching thus the mere hem of his garment, they cannot help believing a little in the man inside the garment.

It is not to be wondered at that such believers should so often be miserable. They lay themselves down to sleep with nothing but the skirt of his robe in their hand—a robe too, I say, that never was his, they only suppose it his—when they might sleep in peace with the living Lord in their hearts.

Instead of so knowing Christ that they have him in them saving them, they lie wasting themselves in soul-sickening self-examination as to whether they are believers, whether they are really trusting in the atonement, whether they are truly sorry for their sins—the way to madness of the brain and despair of the heart. Some even ponder the imponderable—whether they are of the elect, whether they have an interest in the blood shed for sin, whether theirs is a saving faith—when all the time the man who died for them is waiting to begin to save them from every evil—and first from this self which is consuming them with trouble about its salvation.

He will set them free and take them home to the bosom

of the Father, if only they will mind what he says to them—
which is the beginning, middle, and end of faith. If, instead of
searching into the mysteries of corruption in their own char-
nel house, they would but awake and arise from the dead, and
come out into the light which Christ is waiting to give them,
he would begin at once to fill them with the fullness of God.

It Is Obedience

"But I do not know how to awake and arise."

I will tell you: Get up and do something the Master tells
you. In such a manner you will make yourself his disciple at
once. Instead of asking whether you believe or not, ask yourself whether you have this day done one thing because he
said, *Do it*, or once abstained because he said, *Do not do it*.

It is simply absurd to say you believe, or even want to
believe in him, if you do not do anything he tells you. If you
can think of nothing he ever said as having had an atom of
influence on your *doing* or *not doing*, you have no good ground
to consider yourself a disciple of his. Do not, I implore you,
worse than waste your time in trying to convince yourself that
you *are* his disciple and that for this reason or that you can be
sure that you believe in him. Even though you might be able
to succeed in persuading yourself to absolute certainty that
you are his disciple, what difference will it make if one day
he says to you, "Why did you not do the things I told you?
Depart from me—I do not know you!"

Do not try to persuade yourself. If the thing be true you

can make it truer. If it be not true, you can begin at once to make it true, to *be* a disciple of the Living One—by obeying him in the first thing you can think of in which you are not obeying him.

We must learn to obey him in everything, and so must begin somewhere. Let it be at once, and in the very next thing that lies at the door of our conscience!

Oh, fools and slow of heart, if you think of nothing but Christ and do not set yourselves to do his words! You but build your houses on the sand. What will the religious teachers have to answer for who have turned your regard away from the direct words of the Lord himself, which are spirit and life, to contemplate instead various plans of salvation tortured out of the words of his apostles, even if those plans were as true as they are actually false! There is but one plan of salvation, and that is to believe in the Lord Jesus Christ— that is, to take him for what he is, our Master, and his words as if he meant them, which assuredly he did.

To do his words is to enter into vital relationship with him. To obey him is the only way to be one with him. The relationship between him and us is an absolute one. It can begin to *live* no way but in obedience. It *is* obedience.

There can be no truth, no reality, in any initiation of at-one-ment with him that is not obedience.

Will one with even the poorest notion of a God dare think of entering into relationship with him and ignore the very first principle of such relationship, which is: *What he says I will do?* The thing is eternally absurd and comes from the father of lies.

I know what he whispers to those of you to whom my words are distasteful: "He is teaching the doctrine of works!"

But one word of the Lord humbly heard and received will suffice to send all the demons of false theology into the abyss. He says the man who does not do the things he tells him builds his house to fall in utter ruin. He instructs his messengers to go and baptize all nations, "teaching them to observe all things whatsoever I have commanded you."

Tell me it is faith he requires—I know it! And is not faith the highest act of which the human mind is capable? But faith in what? Faith in what he is, in what he says—a faith which can have no existence except in obedience—a faith which *is* obedience. To do what he wishes is to put forth faith in him.

WHAT IS TRUE FAITH?

For this the teaching of men has substituted this or that belief *about* him, faith in this or that supposed design of his manifestation in the flesh. It was himself, and God in him, that he manifested. But faith in him and his Father thus manifested, they make altogether secondary to acceptance of the paltry contrivance of a juggling morality, which they attribute to God and his Christ, imagining it the atonement and "the plan of salvation."

"Do you put faith in *him*," I ask, "or in the doctrines and commandments of men?"

If you say "in him," then I return with this question: "Is it possible that you do not see that, above all things and all thoughts, you are bound to obey him?" Do you not express longing to trust in him more but find it too hard? Too hard it is for you, and too hard it will remain while the things he tells you to do—the things you can do—even those you will not try!

How should you be capable of trusting in the true one while you are not true to him? How are you to believe he will do his part by you while you are not such as to do your part by him? How are you to believe while you are not faithful? How, I say, should you be capable of trusting in him? The very thing that will make you able to trust in him, and thus able to receive all things from him, you turn your back upon. Obedience you decline, or at least neglect.

You say you do not refuse to obey him? I care not whether you refuse or not, while you do not obey. Remember the parable: "I go, sir, and went not." What have you done *this day* because it was the will of Christ? Have you once dismissed an anxious thought for the morrow? Have you ministered to any needy soul or body and kept your right hand from knowing what your left hand did? Have you begun to leave all and follow him? Did you set yourself to judge righteous judgment? Are you being wary of covetousness? Have you forgiven your enemy? Are you seeking the kingdom of God and his righteousness before all other things? Are you hungering and thirsting after righteousness? Have you given to someone that asked of you? Tell me something that you have done, are doing, or are trying to do because he told you.

If you do nothing that he says, it is no wonder that you cannot trust in him and are therefore driven to seek refuge in the atonement as if something he had done, and not he himself in his doing were the atonement.

Is that not how you understand it? What does it matter how you understand, or what you understand, so long as you are not of one mind with the Truth, so long as you and God are not *at one*, do not atone together? How should you understand? Knowing that you do not heed his Word, why should I heed your explanation of it? You do not his will, and so you cannot understand him. You do not know him, and that is why you cannot trust in him. You think your common sense enough to let you know what he means? Your common sense ought to be enough to know itself unequal to the task. It is the heart of the child that alone can understand the Father.

Would you have me think you guilty of the sin against the Holy Ghost—that you *understand* Jesus Christ and yet will not obey him? That would be too dreadful. I believe you do not understand him. No man can do yet what he tells him aright—but are you trying? Obedience is not perfection, but trying.

You count him a hard master, and will not stir. Do you suppose he ever gave a commandment knowing it was of no use for it could not be done? He tells us a thing knowing that we must do it or be lost. He knows that not even his Father himself could save us but by getting us at length to do everything he commands. There is no other way we can know life or learn the holy secret of divine being.

He knows that you can try, and that in your trying and failing he will be able to help you, until at length you shall do the will of God even as he does it himself. He takes the will in the imperfect deed and makes the deed at last perfect.

Correctest notions without obedience are worthless. The doing of the will of God is the way to oneness with God, which alone is salvation. Sitting at the gate of heaven, sitting on the footstool of the throne itself—yea, clasping the very knees of the Father—you could not be at peace, except in their every vital movement, in their smallest point of consciousness, your heart, your soul, your mind, your brain, your body, were one with the living God.

If you had one brooding thought that was not a joy in him, you would not be at peace. If you had one desire you could not leave absolutely to his will, you would not be at peace. You would not be saved, therefore could not feel saved. God, all and in all, ours to the fulfilling of our very being, is the religion of the perfect, son-hearted Lord Christ.

PAGANISM PERSISTS IN
LOW INTERPRETATIONS OF GOD'S WAYS

Of course I know it is faith that saves us. But it is not faith in any work of God—it is faith in God himself. If I did not believe God is as good as the tenderest human heart—as good as the fairest, purest, most unselfish human heart could imagine him, yea, an infinitude better, higher than we as the heavens are higher than the earth, believe it, not as a mere theory or proposition, or even as a thing I was intellectually convinced of, but with the responsive condition and being of my whole nature—then what would faith really mean? If I did not feel every fibre of heart and brain and body safe with him because he is the Father who made me as I am, I would not be saved. For this faith is salvation. It is God and the man as one. God and man together, the vital energy flowing unchecked from the creator into his creature—that is the salvation of the creature.

But the poorest faith in the living God, the God revealed in Christ Jesus—if it be vital and true, that is, obedient—is the beginning of the way to know him. And to know him is eternal life. If you mean by faith anything of a different kind, that faith will not save you. A faith, for instance, that God does not forgive me because he loves me, but because he loves Jesus Christ, cannot save me. It is a falsehood against God. If the thing were true, such a gospel would be the preaching of a God that was not love, therefore in whom was no salvation, a God whom to know could not be eternal life. Such a faith would damn, not save a man, for it would bind him to a God who was anything but perfect.

Such assertions going by the name of Christianity are nothing but the poor remnants of paganism. It is only with that part of our nature not yet Christian that we are able to believe them, so far indeed as it is possible a lie should be believed at all.

We must forsake all our fears and distrusts for Christ. We must receive his teaching heartily and not let the interpretation of it attributed to his apostles make us turn aside from it. I say *interpretation* attributed to them, for what they teach is never against what Christ taught, though very often the exposition of it is. This comes from no fault in the apostles but from the grievous fault of those who would understand, and even explain, rather than obey.

We may be sure of this, that no man will be condemned for any sin that is past. If he be condemned it will be because he would not come to the light when the light came to him, because he would not cease to do evil and learn to do well. The only things that will be held against him will be that he hid his unbelief in the garment of a false faith and would not obey, that he imputed to himself a righteousness that was not his, that he preferred imagining himself a worthy person to confessing himself everywhere in the wrong and repenting.

We may be sure also of this, that if a man becomes the disciple of Christ, the Lord will not leave him in ignorance as to what he has to believe. He shall know the truth of everything it is needful for him to understand. If we do what he tells us, his light will go up in our hearts. Till then we could not understand even if he explained to us. If you cannot trust him to let you know what is right, but think you must hold this or that doctrine before you can come to him, then your occasional doubts probably give rise to what are actually your best times spiritually, in which you come nearest to the truth—those, namely, in which you fear you have no faith.

So long as a man will not set himself to obey the word spoken, the word written, the word printed, the word read, of the Lord Christ, I would not take the trouble to convince him concerning the most obnoxious doctrines that they are false as hell. It is those who want to believe but who are hindered from true belief by such doctrines whom I would help. Disputation about things but hides the living Christ who alone can teach the truth, who is the truth, and the knowledge of whom is life.

I write for the sake of those driven away from God by false teaching that claims to be true. And well it might drive them away, for the god so taught by some of those doctrines is not a god worthy to be believed in. A stick, or a stone, or a devil, is all that some of our brethren of mankind have to believe in. He who believes in a god not altogether unselfish and good, a god who does not do all he can for his creatures, belongs to the same class. His is not the God who made the heaven and the earth and the sea and the fountains of water— not the God revealed in Christ.

If a man see in God any darkness at all, and especially if he defend that darkness according to his contorted theologies, attempting to justify it by saying that he is one who respects the person of God, I cannot but think his blindness must follow his mockery of *"Lord! Lord!"* Surely, if he had been strenuously obeying Jesus, he would before now have received the truth that God is light, and in him is no darkness—a truth which is not acknowledged by calling the darkness attributed to him light, and the candle of the Lord in the soul of man darkness. It is one thing to believe that God can do nothing wrong, quite another to call whatever presumption may attribute to him right.

ONLY AS WE DO CAN WE KNOW

The whole secret of progress is the doing of the thing we know. There is no other way of progress in the spiritual life, no other way of progress in the understanding of that life. Only as we *do* can we *know*.

Is there then anything you will not leave for Christ? You cannot know him—and yet he is the Truth, the one thing alone that can be known!

Do you not care that you are imperfect? Would you rather keep this or that imperfection than part with it to be perfect? You cannot know Christ, for the very principle of his life was the simple, absolute relation of realities—his one idea was to be a perfect child to his Father.

He who will not part with all for Christ is not worthy of him and cannot know him. The Lord is true and cannot acknowledge such a one. How could he receive to his house, as one of his kind, a man who prefers something to his Father, a man who is not wholly *for* God, a man who will strike a bargain with God and say, "I will give up so much, if you will spare me."

Such a man or woman counts it too much to yield all to him who has only made us and given us everything, yea his very self by life and by death. His conduct says, "I never asked you to do so much for me, and I cannot make the return you demand." He will have to be left to himself. He must find what it is to be without God!

Those, on the other hand, who *do* know God—or have but begun to catch a far-off glimmer of his gloriousness, of what he is—regard life as insupportable except that God be the all in all, the first and the last.

HOW THE WORLD WOULD BE CHANGED
IF WE ONLY OBEYED!

To let their light shine, not to force on them their interpretations of God's designs, is the duty of Christians toward their fellows.

If you who set yourselves to explain the theory of Christianity had set yourselves instead to do the will of the Master, the one object for which the gospel was preached to you, how different would now be the condition of that portion of the world with which you come into contact! Had you given yourselves to the understanding of his Word that you might do it, and not to the quarrying from it of material wherewith to buttress your systems, in many a heart by this time would the name of the Lord be loved where now it remains unknown.

The word of life would then have been held out to a hungry world indeed!

Attracted by your behaviour and undeterred by your explanations of Christianity—for you would not be forcing them on their acceptance—men and women would be saying to each other, as Moses said to himself when he saw the bush that burned with fire and was not consumed, "I will now turn aside and see this great sight!"

All around you they would be drawing nigh to behold how these Christians loved one another!

They would see how just and fair Christians were to every one that had to do with them. They would take note that their goods were the best, their weight surest, their prices most reasonable, their word most certain. They would see in their families neither jealousy nor emulation, that mammon was not worshiped, that in their homes selfishness was neither the hidden nor the openly ruling principle. They would see that their children were as diligently taught to share as some are to save or to spend upon self. They would see that their mothers were more anxious lest a child should hoard than lest he should squander. They would see that in no Christian house was religion one thing while in the practice of daily life another, and that among them the ecclesiastic did not think first of his church nor the peer of his privileges.

FALSE FAITH AND TRUE FAITH

What do I hear you say in objection? *"How could the world go on if people lived so?"*

The Lord's world will go on, and perhaps without you. The devil's world will go on too, and may include you. Your objection is but another and overwhelming proof of your unbelief. Either you do not believe the word the Lord spoke—that, if we seek first the kingdom of God and his righteousness, all things we need will be added to us—or what he undertakes does not satisfy you. It is not enough. You want more. You prefer the offers of mammon.

You are in no way anxious to be saved from the snare of *too-much*. You want what you call a fortune—the freedom of the world. You do not want to live under such restrictions as the Lord might choose to lay upon you if he saw that something might be made of you precious in his sight! You want to inherit the earth, but not by meekness. You want to have the comforts of the life of this world, come what may of life eternal, the life that God shares with you. Whatever will happen with regard to that you would gladly let God look after, if only you might be sure of not sharing the fate of the rich man when you die.

But you find that, unable to trust him for this world, neither can you trust him for the world to come. Refusing to obey him in your life, how can you trust him for your life? Hence the various substitutes you seek for faith in him.

You would hold him to his word, bind him by his promises, appeal to the atonement, to the satisfaction made to his justice, as you call it. But all the while you take no trouble to fulfill the morally and spiritually imperative condition—the condition and means in one—on which he gives life to those who believe in, that is, obey, him. Only through this absolutely reasonable and necessary condition can he offer you deliverance from the burden of life into the strength and glory of life—that you shall be true, and to him, obedient children.

You say, "Christ has satisfied the law," but you will not satisfy him!

He says, "Come unto me," and you will not rise and go to him.

You say, "Lord I believe; help mine unbelief." But when he says, "Leave everything behind you and be as I am toward God, and you shall have peace and rest," you turn away, muttering about *figurative language.*

If you had been true, had been living *the* life, had been

Christians indeed, you would, however little, have drawn the world after you. In your churches you would be receiving truest nourishment, yea strength to live—thinking far less of serving God on the Sunday and far more of serving your neighbour during the week. The sociable vile, the masterful rich, the deceitful trader, the ambitious poor, whom you have attracted to your communities with the offer of a salvation other than deliverance from sin, would not be lording it over them and dragging those neighbours down. Your churches would be the cleaner and the stronger for their absence.

Meanwhile, the publicans and sinners would have been drawn instead, and turned into true men and women. And the Israelite indeed, who is yet more repelled by your general worldliness than by your misrepresentations of God that show him selfish like yourselves rather than the purity of creation—the Israelite in whom is no guile would have hastened to the company of the loving men and true, eager to learn what it was that made them so good, so happy, so unselfish, so free of care, so ready to die, so willing to live, so hopeful, so helpful, so careless to possess, so un-deferential to possession.

Finding you to hold—from the traditional force of false teaching—such things as you do, he would have said, "No—such beliefs can never account for such mighty results!"

You would have answered, "Search the Scriptures and see."

He would have searched, and found—not indeed the things you imagine there, but things infinitely better and higher, things that indeed account for the result he marveled at. He would have found such truth as he who has found will hold forever as the only gladness of his being. There you would have had your reward for being true Christians in spite of the evil doctrines you had been taught and teaching. You would have been taught in return the truth of the matter by him whom your true Christianity had enticed to itself, and sent to the fountainhead free of the prejudices that disabled your judgment.

Thus delivered from the false notions which could not fail to have stunted your growth hitherto, how rapid would it now have become!

IN DOING RIGHT WILL WE THINK RIGHT?

If any of you tell me my doctrine is presumptuous, that it is contrary to what is taught in the New Testament and what the best of theologians have always believed, I will not therefore proceed to defend my beliefs and these principles on which I try to live. How much less will I defend my opinions!

I appeal to you instead by asking whether or not I have spoken the truth concerning our paramount obligation to *do* the word of Christ.

If you answer that I have not, I have nothing more to say. There is no other ground on which we can meet. But if you agree that it *is* a prime—even if you do not allow it *the* prime duty—then what I insist upon is that you should do it. Thus and not on any other basis may we recommend the knowledge of him.

I do not attempt to change your opinions. If they are wrong, the obedience alone on which I insist can enable you to set them right. I only urge you to obey, and assert that thus only can you fit yourselves for understanding the mind of Christ.

I say none but he who does right can think right. You cannot *know* Christ to be right until you do as he does and as he tells you to do. Neither can you set him forth to others until you know him as he means himself to be known—that is, as he is.

If you are serving and trusting in mammon, how can you know the living God, the source of life, who is alone to be trusted in? If you do not admit that it is the duty of a man to do the word of Christ, or if, admitting the duty, you yet do not care to perform it, why should I care to convince you that my doctrine is right?

What is it to any true man what you think of his doctrine? What does it matter what you think of any doctrine? If I could convince the judgment of your intellects, your hearts remaining as they are, I should but add to your condemnation.

The true heart must see at once, that, however wrong I may or may not be in other things, at least I am right in this—that Jesus must be obeyed, and obeyed immediately, in the things he did say. The true heart will not long imagine to obey him in things he did not say. If a man does what is unpleasing to Christ, believing it his will, he shall yet gain thereby, for it gives the Lord a hold of him, which he will use. But before he can reach liberty, he must be delivered from that falsehood.

For him who does not choose to see that Christ must be

obeyed, he must be left to the teaching of the Father, who brings all that hear and learn of him to Christ that they may learn what he is who has taught them and brought them. He will leave no man to his own way, however much he may prefer it.

The Lord did not die to provide a man with the wretched heaven he may invent for himself or accept invented for him by others. He died to give him life and bring him to the heaven of the Father's peace. The children must share in the essential bliss of the Father and the Son.

This is and has been the Father's work from the beginning—to bring us into the home of his heart, where he shares the glories of life with the Living One, in whom was born life to light men back to the original life. This is our destiny. And however a man may refuse, he will find it hard to fight with God—useless to kick against the goads of his love. For the Father is goading him, or will goad him, if needful, into life by unrest and trouble. Hellfire itself will have its turn if less will not do.

Can any need it more than such as will neither enter the kingdom of heaven themselves, nor allow those who would to enter it? The old race of the Pharisees is by no means extinct. They were St. Paul's great trouble and are yet to be found in every religious community under the sun.

WHEN WE WALK IN THE LIGHT, TRUTH WILL GROW

The only thing that will truly reconcile all differences is this: To walk in the light. So St. Paul teaches us in his epistle

80 — THE TRUTH IN JESUS

to the Philippians, the third chapter and sixteenth verse.

After setting forth the loftiest idea of human endeavour in declaring the summit of his own aspiration, he does not say, "This must be your endeavour also, or you cannot be saved." Rather he says, "If in anything ye be otherwise minded, God shall reveal even this unto you. Nevertheless whereto we have already attained, let us walk by that same."

Observe what widest conceivable scope is given by the apostle to honest opinion, even in things of grandest import! The only essential point with him is that whereto we have attained, what we have seen to be true, *we walk by that*. In such walking, and in such walking only, love will grow and truth will grow. The soul, then, first in its genuine element and true relation toward God, will see into reality what was before but a blank to it. And he who has promised to teach will teach abundantly.

Faster and faster will the glory of the Lord dawn upon the hearts and minds of his people so walking. Then they will be his people indeed! Fast and far will the knowledge of him spread. Truth of action, both preceding and following truth of word, will prepare the way before him.

The man who walks in that to which he has attained—that truth he has been shown—will be able to think aright. The man who does not think right *cannot* think right because he has not been walking right. Only when he begins to do the thing he knows will he begin to think aright. Then God will come to him in a new and higher way, and work along with the spirit he has created. Without its heaven above its head, without its life breath around it, without its love treasure in its heart, without its origin one with it and bound up in it, without its true self and originating life, no human soul can think to any real purpose—nor ever could to all eternity.

When man joins with God, then is all impotence and discord cast out. Until then, there can be but disharmony. God is constantly working against the gates of hell that open in the heart of man. He can but hold his own as long as the man contests against him. But when the man *joins* God in the battle, then is Satan foiled. For then, for the first time, nature receives her necessity—no such necessity does she have so fundamental as this law of all laws—that God and man are one. Until they begin to be one in the *reality* as they have always been in the divine idea—in the flower as in the root, in the finishing as in the issuing creation—nothing can go right with the man, and God can have no rest from his labour in him.

As the greatest orbs in heaven are drawn by the least, God himself must be held in divine disquiet until every one of his family be brought home to his heart. There they will become one with him in a unity too absolute, profound, far-reaching, fine, and intense to be understood by any but the God from whom such unity comes. Such a high reconciliation is to be guessed at, however, by the soul from the unspeakableness of its delight when at length it is with the *only* one that can be its own, the one that it can possess, the One that can possess it.

For God is the heritage of the soul in the *ownness* of origin. Man is the offspring of his making will, of his life. God himself is his birthplace. God is the self that makes the soul able to say, *I too, I myself*. This absolute unspeakable bliss of the creature is that for which the Son died, for which the Father suffered with him. Then only is life itself. Then only is it right, is it one. Then only is it as designed and necessitated by the eternal life-outgiving Life.

Whereto then we have attained, let us *walk* by that same!

Insights Into

THE TRUTH IN JESUS

Michael Phillips

In MacDonald's novel *There and Back* (*The Baron's Apprenticeship* in THE NEW CLASSICS series), a recurring theme concerns the nature of the God we believe in. To the question posed by the young doubting Barbara Wilder, "Do you think it very bad of a man not to believe in God?" Mac-Donald's Thomas Wingfold answers: "That depends on the sort of God he imagines that he either does or does not believe in. . . . When one looks at the gods that have been offered through the years who are not worth believing in, it might be an act of virtue not to believe in them."

For MacDonald, all faith in God—indeed, everything in

life—hinged on how true was one's understanding of God's being and character. In one sense, his whole life can be seen as an attempt to clear away wrong conceptions in order that an accurate image of God's true nature might emerge.

In the above novel, MacDonald says of another character:

> From an early age Richard had been accustomed to despise the form he called God which stood in the gallery of his imagination, carved at by the hands of successive generations of sculptors—some hard, some feeble, some clever, some stupid, all conventional and without prophetic imagination. . . . The human niche, where the ideas of God must stand, was in Richard's house occupied with the most hideous of falsity. . . . For when a thoughtful man knows nothing of God's nature of devoted fatherhood, it is more than natural for him to recoil from his lesser notions of God.

Later, in the thoughts of this same Richard Tuke, MacDonald repeats a variation of Wingfold's comment to Barbara: "Everything depended on the kind of God believed in . . . how many ideas of God might there be . . . some of them might be nearer right than others."

With a question pointing to that same theme which permeates his work, MacDonald begins his sermon entitled "The Truth in Jesus" (*Unspoken Sermons, Second Series*):

"How have we learned Christ?"

He replies that it is a startling thought that we may have learned him wrong. But then he makes an even more startling assertion, which we saw in Wingfold's words—that it would be better *not* to have learned him at all than to think we know him but not know him as he truly is . . . in other words, to worship a false Christ. In MacDonald's estimation, this is exactly the position of a great many of those calling themselves Christians.

> Throughout its history, the Christian faith has been open to more corrupt misrepresentation than the Jewish could ever be. As it is higher and wider, so must it yield larger scope to corruption. Have we learned of Christ in false statements and corrupted lessons about him, or have we learned *himself?*

GEORGE MACDONALD'S MISSION

MacDonald lived in an era not unlike our own—indeed, not unlike all eras in this respect—when the images harbored, as he says, in the gallery of men's imaginations, about God, Jesus, God's work and character, and about many doctrines and diverse aspects of the Christian faith, were for the most part images and ideas handed down by the traditions of those who had come before—*some hard, some feeble, some clever, some stupid, all conventional and without prophetic imagination.*

Few Christians, as he saw it, took it upon themselves to think rigorously about what they believed, to consider the implications of those beliefs, to square those beliefs with what must be the true character of God. Most, rather, were content to take what they had received about God and his ways and the doctrines upon which their churches were based, without pausing to consider at what points those doctrines may not have been credible.

According to MacDonald, we have learned—or perhaps it should be said, we have been taught—inaccurate, unscriptural, inconsistent, and false ideas about God. Or, in the terms of this particular address, *we have learned Christ wrong.*

In one sense, it might be said that this single fact lay at the root and foundation of George MacDonald's life and writing ministry. It gave impetus and energy to the urge, the dedication, the vision, the imperative calling he felt throughout his life to inform and teach and illuminate and awaken Christians *aright* about God, to stir in the hearts of his readers the hunger to look up into God's face for themselves, there to discover the *Abba* of Jesus Christ whom they might learn to call by that most precious of all names . . . *Father!*

This "mission," as his son Ronald termed it, obviously contained a negative component. First, centuries-old ingrained inaccurate perspectives and images based on false doctrines and misinterpretations of Scripture had to be dismantled. Then MacDonald in a sense had to introduce his readers afresh to the God he had himself come to know—for them a new God, but in fact the *true* God of the Bible, the God of the universe, the God of nature, the *Abba* of intimacy, the Father of Jesus Christ.

The perceptive reader can discern this twofold objective in nearly everything MacDonald wrote—every story, every sermon, even every fairy tale. It is there in *North Wind* as

North Wind explains to Diamond why she must sink the ship. It is prominent in *Lilith*. It radiates out of the Curdie books. It figures into the growth of every character of every novel. And nowhere do we see it more clearly than in the character of Richard Tuke of *There and Back*, who must first dismantle false images in order that he may come to believe in the true God . . . believe in God as he *really* is.

This dual emphasis was clarified in a talk given by Adam Mackay in Huntly in 1924, on the centenary of George Mac-Donald's birth. Mackay commented:

> His message . . . is both positive and negative—negative as to many of the dogmas commonly regarded as inviolate in his day; and positive as to the great facts of Christian teaching which have been the heritage of believers in every generation . . . but whether he is destroying dogmas that offend or upholding dogmas that appeal, he invariably finds the conscience of his reader. . . .
>
> George MacDonald of course suffered . . . by having to work through much that was false before he could reach the true. The passage from the negative to positive was in his case both logical in sequence and chronological in time. . . . For keep in mind that during the formative period of George MacDonald's life, a very narrow and a very rigid type of orthodoxy held sway. . . . It was unbending in its sternness to sin, and uncompromising in its treatment of sinners. In short, it produced, as it could only produce, either saints or hypocrites.

A similar though differently directed observation was made by the venerable G. K. Chesterton, also on the centenary of MacDonald's birth (just as this series of books now commemorates the centenary of MacDonald's death). Writing his Introduction to Greville MacDonald's *George MacDonald and His Wife* (1924), Chesterton compared MacDonald to Thomas Carlyle. Both men were raised in the Calvinism of the day. But whereas Carlyle overreacted against the excesses of that Calvinism (as have many, including the author MacDonald quotes in the opening pages of this sermon), MacDonald was energized by his upbringing to search after a deeper, truer faith.

Wrote Chesterton,

The originality of George MacDonald has also a historical significance, which perhaps can best be estimated by comparing him to his great countryman Carlyle. . . . If an escape from the bias of environment be the test of originality, Carlyle never completely escaped, and George MacDonald did. He evolved . . . a completely alternate theology. . . . Carlyle could never have said anything so subtle and simple as MacDonald's saying that God is easy to please and hard to satisfy. Carlyle was too obviously occupied with insisting that God was hard to satisfy; just as some optimists are doubtless too much occupied with insisting that He is easy to please. MacDonald . . . made for himself a sort of spiritual environment, a space and transparency of mystical light. . . . And when he comes to be more carefully studied . . . it will be found, I fancy, that he stands for a rather important turning-point in the history of Christendom, as representing the particular Christian nation of the Scots.

The words of both Mackay and Chesterton possess a common thread: MacDonald's ability to sift the wheat from the chaff, to discern what is *wrong* in accepted orthodoxy in order to discover what is *true* about God.

As simple as it seems, this two-edged sword is rarely wielded with skill. Neither the skeptic nor the dogmatist is usually able to do so. To borrow from Chesterton, the skeptic is too obviously occupied with pointing to what is wrong with orthodoxy, just as the dogmatist is too much occupied with insisting that the orthodoxy is true.

What sets MacDonald apart is his precision with that sword in the cause of truth, as a modern Scot's warrior brandishing his claymore, not in battle against flesh and blood but in spiritual battle against false ideas and false conceptions of God. In the gallery of eternity, it may be MacDonald's portrait that hangs higher in the honor of Scotland's history than that of Wallace, the Bruce, bonny Prince Charlie, and all the rest. For his warfare was waged on behalf of eternal truth, not temporal causes. Like Scotland's heroes of legend, MacDonald also devoted his life to the cause of liberty. Yet his was not a fight for Scottish liberation alone, but for the freedom of all thinking Christians—to liberate them from the constraints of falsely taught dogmas and religious systems.

It is this two-edged sword that he wields here with power and honesty. There is no throwing out of the baby with the bathwater. MacDonald must dismantle the *false* before moving toward discovery of the *true*. His vision is ever piercing and focused—never intent to debunk, dedicated only and uncompromisingly to find *truth*.

Against hypocrisy he will rail, wherever he finds it. He begins briefly with certain observations and challenges to the quoted skeptic, and soon the Christians come in for their own share.

Most acutely of all will his ire raise itself against false-hoods upon Infinite Love. But, as I say, never to debunk, only so that God might be truly *known*, and his Son truly *obeyed*.

A PERSONAL EXPOSITION OF OUTRAGE

In the syntax and style of the time, MacDonald's personal intrusions into his writing are not always immediately obvi-ous. But in this particular sermon we find a miniature auto-biography of faith, in which he speaks of his personal reaction against the Calvinist view of atonement. One can only con-clude that his own spiritual pilgrimage is the basis for what follows. If we have eyes and ears to see and hear it, in this sermon we are presented with one of his most deeply per-sonal utterances. It illuminates much about his own faith, and the paths he trod both intellectually and spiritually to reach it. He uses the unnamed skeptic author as a literary foil to represent the belief system of his own childhood. He then explains the progression by which he came to escape that sys-tem and arrive at what he calls "the truth in Jesus." In this autobiographical sense, as well as for the truth revealed by the two-edged sword of his spiritual wisdom, this must surely be considered one of MacDonald's most important and signifi-cant theological essays.

The increasing boldness throughout his life to speak on spiritually controversial matters is an intriguing though neglected aspect of MacDonald's biography and spiritual development. When "The Truth in Jesus" was first written we cannot know. It was published in 1885, when MacDonald was sixty years of age.

Fifty years earlier he often sat in church in his hometown of Huntly, listening as the very doctrines were expounded that he here addresses. In the intervening years, he first learned to question them. As he grew into a young man he embarked on a personal quest to discover God's true nature. And as manhood overtook him, with maturity came the confidence to speak boldly to those still enmeshed in the crippling theological outlook he had escaped.

He has grown from a boy into a prophet. And, as is true of most prophets, with the confidence that he is indeed speaking on behalf of the true God, came an occasional eruption of outrage at the falsehoods he now perceives clearly.

George MacDonald has come full circle. From the timid child afraid to voice his inner doubts (one remembers the boy Robert Falconer), at sixty he now mounts the pulpit to speak publicly against the entire system of belief.

It is a rather remarkable spiritual progression.

In this "unspoken" sermon, MacDonald employs a technique that he uses frequently but which occasionally renders the literary "flow" of his ideas a little difficult. That is, he engages in imaginary conversation with his reader, voicing possible objections. Then he responds, again in his own voice. In so doing, he does not always set these thoughts or statements apart with consistency—in italics or with quotation marks or with paragraph breaks as would be the case with most written dialogue. Taking the rough with the smooth, however, it is often when he is writing thus that we find George MacDonald at his most personal, his most emotional . . . his most spontaneous and unvarnished.

In the preceding chapter, in MacDonald's sermon entitled "The Truth," we have one of the most well-ordered, cohesive, unified examples of writing to proceed from his pen. Its brilliant content aside, it is simply a magnificently crafted exposition. Every element hangs together and flows *out* of what has come before and *into* what is to come—the whole, precept upon precept, building exquisitely toward the climax.

Such cannot be said for "The Truth in Jesus." It is on the whole disjointed and rambling. Yet that is because it is personal and conversational. Here is MacDonald with the gloves off, so to speak, wearing no pulpit robe of finery, not cautious over every word. Here MacDonald lets himself go. We follow his thoughts as rapidly as they come, in whatever direction they take us.

This whole address feels less like a sermon and more like a group discussion, in which MacDonald is sitting with believers of all stripes—some sincere seekers after truth, others irate at what he says. He fields questions and objections and moves in whatever direction the discussion takes.

Indeed, I have little doubt that he frequently found himself in discussions very much like the one he represents for us here. As one recalls the boy Robert Falconer, one also recalls the youthful MacDonald visiting the home of his future wife,

Louisa, there engaging in many discussions concerning the atonement, orthodoxy on which doctrine was a subject of some "difficulty" between the seminarian MacDonald and the young lady whose hand he hoped to win.

After his initial challenges to the skeptic who has not been intellectually honest enough to investigate the historic veracity of Christianity in depth, MacDonald then gets down to the business at hand:

"I desire to address those who call themselves Christians, and expostulate with them thus:"

And the discussion begins in earnest. As it does, MacDonald is not afraid to let his passions, even his anger, show.

> What I come to and insist upon is, that, supposing your theories right, even suppose they contain all that is to be believed, those theories are not what makes you Christians, if Christians indeed you are. On the contrary, they are, with not a few of you, just what *keeps* you from being Christians. . . .
>
> Small wonder that men such as I quoted at the beginning refuse the Christianity they suppose such "believers" to represent! . . .
>
> It is simply absurd to say you believe, or even want to believe in him, if you do not do anything he tells you. . . . Even though you might be able to succeed in persuading yourself to absolute certainty that you are his disciple, what difference will it make if one day he says to you, "Why did you not do the things I told you? Depart from me—I do not know you!" . . .
>
> Oh, fools and slow of heart, if you think of nothing but

Christ and do not set yourselves to do his words! You but build your houses on the sand. What will the religious teachers have to answer for who have turned your regard away from the direct words of the Lord himself, which are spirit and life, to contemplate instead various plans of salvation tortured out of the words of his apostles, even if those plans were as true as they are actually false! . . .

The Lord's world will go on, and perhaps without you. The devil's world will go on too, and may include you.

DISMANTLING THE FALSE TO DISCOVER THE TRUTH

In order to get at true belief, MacDonald does not set forth his own belief but rather examines the nature of belief itself. How do we come to believe as we do—from opinions and theories passed down by men, or from life as we live it?

It is for MacDonald the most fundamental of questions, one which all too few of those calling themselves Christians have paused to seriously consider.

A man's real belief is that which he lives by. . . . What a man believes is the thing he *does*.

As he goes on, MacDonald does not rail against any single specific point of doctrine but against various plans of salvation and the whole system of belief in an atonement that places Jesus and his Father at odds in the divine economy.

For when you say that to be saved a man must hold this or that, then you are forsaking the living God and his will and putting trust in some notion *about* him or his will. To make my meaning clearer: Some of you say that we must trust in the finished work of Christ. Or you say that our faith must be in the merits of Christ—in the atonement he has made—in the blood he has shed.

All these statements are a simple repudiation of the living Lord, *in whom* we are told to believe. It is his presence with and in us, and our obedience to him, that lifts us out of darkness into light and leads us from the kingdom of Satan into the glorious liberty of the sons of God. No manner or amount of belief *about him* is the faith of the New Testament.

Again comes the personal note, along with the rising of MacDonald's passion.

With such teaching I have had a lifelong acquaintance, and I declare it most miserably false. But I do not now mean to dispute against it. Except the light of the knowledge of the glory of God in the face of Christ Jesus make a man sick of his opinions, he may hold them to doomsday for me.

No opinion, I repeat, is Christianity, and no preaching of any plan of salvation is the preaching of the glorious gospel of the living God. Even if your plan, your theories, were absolutely true, the holding of them with sincerity, the trusting in this or that about Christ, or in anything he did or could do—the trusting in anything but himself, his own living self—is still a delusion.

MacDonald even goes so far as to equate false "Christian" belief with paganism.

> Such assertions going by the name of Christianity are nothing but the poor remnants of paganism. It is only with that part of our nature not yet Christian that we are able to believe them, so far indeed as it is possible a lie should be believed at all.

As the discussion progresses, some of MacDonald's most memorable passages rise off the page to stun us anew with their clarity of wisdom.

> I can find no words strong enough to serve for the weight of this necessity—this obedience. It is the one terrible heresy of the church, that it has always been presenting something else than obedience as faith in Christ. . . .
>
> If you can think of nothing he ever said as having had an atom of influence on your *doing* or *not doing*, you have no good ground to consider yourself a disciple of his. . . .
>
> We must learn to obey him in everything, and so must begin somewhere. Let it be at once, and in the very next thing that lies at the door of our conscience! . . .
>
> There is but one plan of salvation, and that is to believe in the Lord Jesus Christ—that is, to take him for what he is, our Master, and his words as if he meant them, which assuredly he did.
>
> To do his words is to enter into vital relationship with him. To obey him is the only way to be one with him. The relationship between him and us is an absolute one. It can begin to *live* no way but in obedience. It *is* obedience.

There can be no truth, no reality, in any initiation of at-one-ment with him that is not obedience. . . .

If you who set yourselves to explain the theory of Christianity had set yourselves instead to do the will of the Master . . . how different would now be the condition of that portion of the world with which you come into contact! Had you given yourselves to the understanding of his Word that you might do it, and not to the quarrying from it of material wherewith to buttress your systems, in many a heart by this time would the name of the Lord be loved where now it remains unknown. . . .

I do not attempt to change your opinions. If they are wrong, the obedience alone on which I insist can enable you to set them right. I only urge you to obey, and assert that thus only can you fit yourselves for understanding the mind of Christ.

MacDonald is writing to two classes of people—those who are content and self-satisfied in what he calls their gross and obnoxious beliefs . . . and those who are not content with them, whose hearts cry out for something higher. Toward the former his passion continually rises. Toward the latter, he is tender, patient, encouraging.

He knows the struggle, for it is one he himself passed through.

I write for the sake of those driven away from God by false teaching that claims to be true. And well it might drive them away, for the God so taught by some of those doctrines is not a God worthy to be believed in. . . .

The true heart must see at once, that . . . at least I am

right in this—that Jesus must be obeyed, and obeyed immediately, in the things he did say. . . .

The man who walks in that to which he has attained—that truth he has been shown—will be able to think aright.

To such MacDonald addresses the final remarks of his climax, encouraging the honest hearts among his listeners to seek their destiny, their home, the heart of the Father.

This is the truth in Jesus.

This is and has been the Father's work from the beginning—to bring us into the home of his heart. . . . This is our destiny. . . .

For God is the heritage of the soul. . . . God himself is his birthplace. God is the self that makes the soul able to say, *I too, I myself*. This absolute unspeakable bliss of the creature is that for which the Son died, for which the Father suffered with him. Then only is life itself. Then only is it right, is it one.

KINGSHIP

George MacDonald

Art thou a king then? Jesus answered, Thou sayest that I am
a king! To this end was I born, and for this cause came I
into the world, that I should bear witness unto the truth:
every one that is of the truth heareth my voice.

—John 18:37

Kingship:
To Wash the Feet of a Weary Brother

Pilate asks Jesus if he is a king. The question is prompted
by what the Lord had just said concerning his kingdom, closing with the statement that it was not of this world. He now
answers Pilate that he is a king indeed but shows him that his
kingdom is of a very different kind from what is called kingdom in this world.

The rank and rule of this world are uninteresting to him. He might have had them. Calling his disciples to follow him, and his twelve legions of angels to help them, he might soon have driven the Romans into the abyss, piling them on the heap of nations they had tumbled there before them.

What would have been easier for him than thus to have cleared the way for his own rule? Over the subservient world he might then have reigned as the just monarch that was the dream of the Jews—a king such as had never been seen in Israel or elsewhere but had haunted the hopes and longings of poor and rich alike. He might have ruled the world from Jerusalem. He might not merely have dispensed what men call justice, but have compelled atonement.

But he did not care for government. No such kingdom would serve the ends of his Father in heaven, or satisfy his own soul.

What was perfect empire to the Son of God, while he might teach one human being to love his neighbour and be good like his Father! To be a love-helper to one heart, for its joy, and the glory of his Father, was the beginning of true kingship! The Lord would rather wash the feet of his weary brother than be the one and only perfect monarch that ever ruled in the world. It was empire he rejected when he ordered Satan behind him like a dog to his heel. Government, I repeat, was to him flat, stale, unprofitable.

A Kingdom of Kings

Yet the Lord says that he came into the world to be a king? What then is the kingdom over which the Lord cares to reign?

I answer: A kingdom of kings, and no other. A kingdom where every man is a king, there and there only does the Lord care to reign in the name of his Father.

As no king in Europe would care to reign over a cannibal, a savage, or an animal race, so the Lord cares for no kingdom over anything this world calls a nation. A king must rule over his own kind. Jesus is a king by virtue of no conquest, inheritance, or election, but in the right of essential being. And he cares for no subjects but such as are his subjects by the same right. His subjects must be of his own kind, in their very nature and essence kings.

To understand his answer to Pilate, we must see what his kingship consists of. We must see what it is that makes him a king, what manifestation of his essential being gives him a claim to be king.

It is this: The Lord's is a kingdom in which no man seeks to be above another. Ambition is of the dirt of this world's kingdoms. He says, "I am a king, for I was born for the purpose, and I came into the world with the object of bearing witness to the truth. Everyone that is of my kind, that is of the truth, hears my voice. He is a king like me, and is one of my subjects."

Thereupon—as would most Christians nowadays, instead of setting about being true—Pilate requests a definition of truth, a presentation to his intellect in set terms of what the word *truth* means.

Yet instantly—whether knowing his inquiry was useless or intending to resume it when he has set the Lord free—he goes out to the people to tell them he finds no fault in him.

Whatever interpretation we put on his action here, he must be far less to blame than those "Christians" who, instead of setting themselves to be pure "even as he is pure," to be their brother and sister's keeper and to serve God by being honourable in shop and bank and office and market, proceed to "serve" him by going to church, by condemning the opinions of their neighbours, and by teaching others what they do not themselves heed.

Neither Pilate nor they ask the one true question, "How am I to be a true man? How am I to become a man worth being a man?"

The Lord is a king because his life—the life of his thoughts, his imagination, his will, his every smallest action—is true. He is true first to God in that he is altogether his. Then he is true to himself in that he forgets himself altogether. And finally he is true to his fellows in that he will endure anything they do to him, and not cease declaring himself the son and messenger and likeness of God. They will kill him, but it matters not—the truth is as he says!

THE ONE PRINCIPLE OF HELL

Jesus is a king because his business is to bear witness to the truth. What truth? All truth. All right relations throughout the universe.

First of all, he bears witness to the truth that his father is good, perfectly good, and that the crown and joy of life is to desire and do the will of the eternal source of will and of all life. He thus deals the death-blow to the power of hell.

For the one principle of hell is: "I am my own. I am my own king and my own subject. *I* am the centre from which go out my thoughts. *I* am the object and end of my thoughts. My thoughts return back upon *me* as the alpha and omega of life. My own glory is, and ought to be, my chief care. My ambition is to gather the regards of men to the one centre, myself. My pleasure is *my* pleasure. My kingdom is comprised of as many as I can bring to acknowledge my greatness over them. My judgment is the faultless rule of things. It is my right to have what I desire. The more I am all in all to myself, the greater I am. The less I acknowledge debt or obligation to another, the more I close my eyes to the fact that I did not make myself. The more self-sufficing I feel or imagine myself—the greater I am. I will be free with the freedom that consists in doing whatever I am inclined to do, from wherever may come the inclination. To do my *own* will so long as I feel anything to be my will, is to be free, is to live."

To all these principles of hell, or of this world—they are the same thing, and it matters nothing whether they are specifically spoken or defended so long as they are acted upon—the Lord, the king, gives the direct lie.

JESUS' OWN WITNESS

It is as if he said:

"I ought to know what I say, for from all eternity I have been the son of him from whom you come, and whom you call your father, but whom you will not have as your father. I know all he thinks and is. And I say this, that my perfect freedom, my pure individuality, rests on the fact that I have no other will than his.

"My will is all for his will, for his will is right. He is righteousness itself. His very being is love and equity and self-devotion, and he will have his children such as himself— creatures of love, fairness, self-devotion to him and their fellows. I was born to bear witness to the truth—to be in my own person the truth visible, the very likeness and manifestation of the God who is true. My very being is his witness. Every facet of me witnesses him. He is the truth, and I am the truth.

"Kill me, but while I live I say, *Such as I am he is.* If I said I did not know him, I should be a liar. I fear nothing you can do to me. Shall the king who comes to say what is true turn his back for fear of men? My Father is like me. I know it, and I say it. You do not like to hear it because you are not like him. I am low in your eyes, which measure things by their show and outward appearance. Therefore you say I blaspheme. Indeed, I would blaspheme if I said he was such as anything you are capable of imagining him, for you love show and power and the praise of men. I do not, and God is like me. I came into the world to reveal him.

"I am a king because he sent me to bear witness to his truth, and I have done so. Kill me, and I will rise again. You can kill me, but you cannot hold me dead. Death is my servant. You are the slaves of Death because you will not be true and let the truth make you free. Bound, and in your hands, I am free as God, for God is my Father. I know I shall suffer—suffer unto death. But if you knew my Father, you would not wonder that I am ready to die. You would be ready too. He is my strength. My Father is greater than I."

Remember, friends, I said, "It is as if he said." I am daring to present only a shadow of the Lord's witnessing, a shadow surely cast by his deeds and his very words. If I mistake, he will forgive me. I do not fear him. I fear only lest, able to see and write these things, I should fail of witnessing, and myself be, after all, a castaway—no king, but a mere talker, no disciple of Jesus ready to go with him to the death, but an arguer about the truth, a hater of the lies men speak of God, while I myself remain a truth-speaking liar, not a doer of the Word.

We see, then, that the Lord bore his witness to the Truth, to the one God, by standing there and being just what he was before the eyes and the lies of men. The true king is the man who stands up as a true man and speaks the truth, and will die but not lie. The robes of such a king may be rags or purple—it matters neither way. The rags are the more likely, but neither better nor worse than the robes. The Lord was dressed most royally when his robes were a jest, a mockery, a laughter. Of the men who before Christ bore witness to the truth, some were sawn asunder, some subdued kingdoms. It mattered nothing which—they witnessed.

The truth is *God*. The witness to the truth is Jesus. The kingdom of the truth is the hearts of men. The bliss of men is the true God. The thought of God is the truth of everything.

THE WITNESS OF OUR LIFE IS
OUR TRUE RELATION TO GOD

All well-being lies in true relation to God. The one who responds to this with his whole being is of the truth. The one who knows these things, and merely knows them, the one who sees them to be true but does not order life and action, judgment, and love by them, is the worst kind of liar. With hand, foot, and face he casts scorn upon that which his tongue confesses.

Little did the sons of Zebedee and their ambitious mother think what the earthly throne of Christ's glory was which they and she begged they might share. For the king crowned by his witnessing would soon witness to the height of his uttermost argument by hanging upon a cross—like sin, as Paul in his boldness expresses it.

When his witness is treated as a lie, then most he witnesses, for he gives it still. High and lifted up on the throne of his witness, on the cross of his torture, he holds to it: "I and the Father are one."

Every mockery borne in witnessing is a witnessing afresh. Jesus witnessed to the truth infinitely more than had he sat on the throne of the whole earth when Pilate brought him out for the last time, and perhaps made him sit on the judgment-seat in his mockery of kingly garments and royal insignia, saying, "Behold your king!" Just because of those robes and that crown, that sceptre and that throne of ridicule, he was the only real king that ever sat on any throne.

Is every Christian expected to bear witness? A man content to bear no witness to the truth is not in the kingdom of heaven. One who believes must bear witness. One who sees the truth must live witnessing to it.

Is our life, then, a witnessing to the truth? Do we carry ourselves in bank, on farm, in house or shop, in study or room or workshop, as the Lord would, or as the Lord would not?

Are we careful to be true? Do we endeavour to live to the height of our ideas? Or are we mean, self-serving, world-flattering, fawning slaves?

When contempt is cast on the truth, do we smile? When the truth is wronged in our presence, do we make no sign that we hold by it? I do not say we are called upon to *dispute*, and defend with logic and argument, but we are called upon to show that we are on a different side, the side of truth.

But when I say *truth*, I do not mean *opinion*. To treat opinion as if that were truth is grievously to wrong the truth. The soul that loves the truth and tries to be true will know when to speak and when to be silent. But the true man will never look as if he did not care.

We are not bound to say all we think, but we are bound not even to look what we do not think. The girl who said before a company of mocking companions, "I believe in Jesus," bore true witness to her Master, the Truth. And by so witnessing to the truth, light will come into us, for *he is the light, and in him is no darkness at all.*

Insights Into

KINGSHIP

MICHAEL PHILLIPS

From one of MacDonald's longest sermons, we now turn
to one of his briefest, "Kingship," from *Unspoken Sermons,
Third Series*.

The theme of "truth," from the two preceding chapters,
and that of "kingship" are inextricably linked in the character
of Pontius Pilate, who asked Jesus concerning both. As little
as Pilate recognized The Man who actually stood before him,
he was somehow astute enough in the midst of his cruel
regime to ask the right questions. What words have carried
such poignant significance—a significance more eternal than
Pilate could possibly realize—than his eerily prophetic utterance: *Ecce Homo*.

Indeed, for two thousand years the world has beheld this Man, who is more than a man. Still it does not quite know what to do with him any more than Pilate did. The world knows, in a way, who Jesus is even less than did the Jews or Romans of Jerusalem during that pivotal week of history in the first century. Yet still the world *beholds* him . . . and wonders who he is.

The kingship of Jesus Christ is compelling. He compelled Pilate's gaze, uncertainty, and probing questions as he stood in his tattered robes splattered with blood. It is just because the Lord's kingship is so inverted from the world's image of rule that he arrests the world's attention. It is a compelling kingship, commanding the attention and stares and questions and reflections of kings, governors, high priests, and beggars alike.

It is a kingship whose rule exists over a different kingdom. It is a kingdom whose loftiest expression of kingship is servanthood, where to wash the feet of his weary brothers is the duty, the privilege, the joy of the king himself.

To Pilate, of course, such ideas are nonsense. Neither he nor the rest of the world are able to fathom the nature of the kingdom over which Jesus reigns. They cannot understand that servanthood and self-denial, not rule, are the essence of that inverted kingship.

Though full of profound and important ideas, this is not a complicated sermon. MacDonald identifies seven components of the Lord's kingship.

One, it was *otherworldly*.

The question is prompted by what the Lord had just

said concerning his kingdom, closing with the statement that it was not of this world. He now answers Pilate that he is a king indeed, but shows him that his kingdom is of a very different kind from what is called kingdom in this world.

Two, it was *personal*. The Lord's was not a kingship of empire or government or anything to do with the rank and rule of the world in a corporate, national, or organizational sense.

Over the subservient world he might then have reigned as the just monarch that was the dream of the Jews—a king such as had never been seen in Israel or elsewhere. . . . He might have ruled the world from Jerusalem. He might not merely have dispensed what men call justice, but have compelled atonement.

But he did not care for government. No such kingdom would serve the ends of his father in heaven or satisfy his own soul. . . . It was empire he rejected when he ordered Satan behind him like a dog to his heel. Government, I repeat, was to him flat, stale, unprofitable.

Three, *goodness* was its objective. The Lord's was a kingship whose end was to teach its subjects to be good and love their neighbors.

What was perfect empire to the Son of God, while he might teach one human being to love his neighbour and be good like his Father! To be a love-helper to one heart, for its joy, and the glory of his Father, was the beginning of true kingship! The Lord would rather wash the feet of his weary brother than be the one and only perfect monarch that ever ruled in the world.

Four, its foundation was *equality*. It was a kingship not of king *over* subjects, but one in which all are of the same kind, and are equally kings. Ambition, therefore, was to be found nowhere in such a kingdom. There are subjects and there are rulers. He is the ruler; his subjects are his subjects. But they are all kings together.

> What then is the kingdom over which the Lord cares to reign? . . .
> A kingdom of kings, and no other. A kingdom where every man is a king. . . .
> A king must rule over his own kind. Jesus is a king by virtue of no conquest, inheritance, or election, but in the right of essential being. And he cares for no subjects but such as are his subjects by the same right. His subjects must be of his own kind, in their very nature and essence kings. . . .
> The Lord's is a kingdom in which no man seeks to be above another. Ambition is of the dirt of this world's kingdoms. . . . "Everyone that is of my kind, that is of the truth, hears my voice. He is a king like me, and is one of my subjects."

Five, it was undergirded by *truth*. It was a kingship whose business was to bear witness to the truth.

> The Lord is a king because his life—the life of his thoughts, his imagination, his will, his every smallest action—is true. He is true first to God. . . . Then he is true to himself. . . . And finally he is true to his fellows. . . .

Jesus is a king because his business is to bear witness
to the truth. What truth? All truth. . . .

First of all he bears witness to the truth that his Father
is good, perfectly good, and that the crown and joy of life
is to desire and do the will of the eternal source of will,
and of all life.

Six, it was ruled by the *will of Another.* The Lord's was a
kingship whose king has no will or ambition of his own but
whose will is to do the will of his Father.

"I say this, that my perfect freedom, my pure individuality, rests on the fact that I have no other will than his.

"My will is all for his will, for his will is right. . . .
Every facet of me witnesses him. He is the truth, and I
am the truth. . . .

"I am a king because he sent me to bear witness to
his truth, and I have done so. . . . My Father is greater
than I."

. . . The Lord bore his witness to the Truth, to the one
God, by standing there and being just what he was before
the eyes and the lies of men. The true king is the man
who stands up as a true man and speaks the truth, and
will die but not lie.

Seven, it was a kingdom of the *heart.* It was a kingship
whose kingdom was the hearts of men.

The truth is *God.* The witness to the truth is Jesus.
The kingdom of the truth is the hearts of men. The bliss
of men is the true God. The thought of God is the truth
of everything.

MacDonald concludes, as he always does, by turning the Lord's example toward we who are his followers.

Are we ambitious to rise in the world?

Do we seek to be above another?

Do we carry ourselves as the Lord would carry himself?

Do we speak the truth?

Do we witness to the truth in all we do?

Are we true to our beliefs?

> Is our life, then, a witnessing to the truth? Do we carry ourselves in bank, on farm, in house or shop, in study or room or workshop, as the Lord would, or as the Lord would not?
>
> Are we careful to be true? Do we endeavour to live to the height of our ideas? . . .
>
> When the truth is wronged in our presence, do we make no sign that we hold by it? . . .
>
> The soul that loves the truth and tries to be true will know when to speak and when to be silent. But the true man will never look as if he did not care.

In other words, how faithful are we to the same witness to which Jesus, the truth, bore witness? For though we are his subjects, we are also called to kingship with him.

It is a kingship that ultimately brought Jesus before Pilate, and it is a kingship that will bring us before the witness we have given to truth by our lives.

LIGHT

GEORGE MACDONALD

*This then is the message which we have heard of him, and
declare unto you, that God is light, and in him
is no darkness at all.*
—1 JOHN 1:5
*And this is the condemnation, that light is come into the
world, and men loved darkness rather than light,
because their deeds were evil.*
—John 3:19

We call the story of Jesus, told so differently yet to my
mind so consistently by four narrators, *the gospel.*

What makes this tale *the good news?*

Is everything in the story of Christ's life on earth good
news? Is it good news that the one and only good man ever to
have lived was served by his fellowmen as Jesus was—cast out

of the world in torture and shame? Is it good news that he came to his own, and his own received him not?

What makes it fit, I repeat, to call the tale *good news?*

THAT CALLED A "GOSPEL" WHICH IS THE OPPOSITE OF GOOD NEWS

If we asked this or that theologian, insofar as he was a true man and answered from his own heart and not from the tradition of the elders, we should understand what he saw in it that made it good news to him, though it might involve what would be anything but good news to some of us.

The so-called "deliverance" some think it brings might be founded on such notions of God as to not a few of us contain as little of good as of news. To share in the deliverance which some men find in what they call the gospel—for all do not apply the word to the tale itself, but to certain deductions made from the epistles and their own consciousness of evil— we should have to believe such things of God as would be the opposite of an evangel to us. Indeed, it would be a message from hell itself.

To believe such things, we should have to imagine possibilities worse than any evil from which their "good news" might offer us deliverance. We would first have to believe in an unjust God from whom we have to seek refuge. True, he is called "just" by those holding to such theologies. But at the same time they say he does that which seems to the best in me the essence of *injustice.*

Hearing such a statement, they will tell me that I judge after the flesh.

I answer, "Is it then to the flesh the Lord appeals when he says, *Yea, and why even of yourselves judge ye not what is right?* Is he not the light that lighteth every man that cometh into the world?"

They tell me I was born in sin, and I know it to be true. They tell me also that I am judged with the same severity as if I had been born in righteousness, and that I know to be false. They make it a consequence of the purity and justice of God that he will judge us—born in evil, and for which birth we were not accountable—by our sinfulness instead of by our guilt.

They tell me, or at least give me to understand, that every wrong thing I have done makes me subject to be treated as if I had done that thing with the free will of one who had in him no taint of evil, even though at the time I may not have recognized the thing as evil, or seen it only in the vaguest fashion.

Is there any gospel in telling me that God is unjust but that there is a way of deliverance from him? Show me my God unjust, and you wake in me a damnation from which no power can deliver me—least of all God himself. It may be "good news" to such as are content to have a God capable of unrighteousness, if only he be on *their* side!

THE LORD IS THE GOSPEL

Who would not rejoice to hear from Matthew, Mark, or Luke, what he meant by the word *gospel*—or rather, what in the story of Jesus made him call it *good news*! Each would probably give a different answer to the question, all the answers consistent, and each a germ from which the others might be reasoned. But in the case of John, we do have his answer to the question. He gives us in one sentence of two parts, not indeed the gospel according to John, but the gospel according to Jesus Christ himself.

He had often told the story of Jesus, the good news of what he was, did, and said. What in it did John look upon as the essence of the goodness of its news? In his gospel he now tells us what in it makes it good news—and tells us the very goodness of that good news. It is not his own message about Jesus but the soul of that message which makes it gospel. It is the news Jesus brought *concerning the Father*. That is the message he gave to the disciples to deliver to men.

Throughout the story, in all he does and is and says, Jesus is telling the news concerning his Father. This he was sent to give to John and his companions that they might hand it on to their brothers. But here, in so many words, John tells us what he himself has heard from the Word—what he has gathered from Jesus as the message he has to declare. He has received it in no systematic form. It is what a life, *the* life, what a man, *the* man, has taught him: The Word is the Lord. The Lord is the gospel. The good news is no fagot of sticks of man's gathering on the Sabbath.

Every man must read the Word for himself. One may read it in one shape, another in another. All will be right if it be indeed the Word they read, and if they read it by the lamp of obedience. He who is willing to do the will of the Father shall know the truth of the teaching of Jesus. The spirit is "given to them that obey him."

Let us hear how John reads the Word in his version of the gospel.

"This then is the message," he says, "which we have heard of him, and declare unto you, that God is light, and in him is no darkness at all."

Ah, my heart, this is indeed the good news! This is a gospel!

If God be light, what more, what else can I seek than God, than God himself! Away with your doctrines! Away with your salvation from the "justice" of a God whom it is a horror to imagine! Away with your iron cages of false meta- physics! I am saved—for God is light!

My God, I come to thee. That thou shouldst be thyself is enough for time and eternity, for my soul and all its endless need.

GOD IS LIGHT!

Whatever seems to me darkness, that I will not believe of my God. If I should mistake, and call that darkness which is light, will he not reveal the matter to me, setting it in the light that lighteth every man, showing me that I saw but the husk of the thing, not the kernel? Will he not break open the shell for me, and let the truth of it, his thought, stream out upon me?

He will not let it hurt me to mistake the light for darkness as long as I do not take it and call darkness light. The one comes from blindness of the intellect, the other from blindness of heart and will. I love the light, and will not, at the word of any man or upon the conviction of any man, believe that that which seems to me darkness can exist in God.

Where would the good news be if John said, "God is light, but you cannot see his light. You cannot tell, you have no notion, what light is. What God means by light is not what you mean by light. What God calls light may be horrible darkness to you, for you are of another nature from him!"

Where, I say, would be the good news of that?

It is true that the light of God may be so bright that we see nothing. But that is not darkness, it is infinite hope of light. It is true also that to the wicked "the day of the Lord is darkness, and not light." But is that because the conscience of the wicked man judges good and evil oppositely to the conscience of the good man? I think not. When he says, "Evil, be thou my good" he means by *evil* the same thing that God means by evil, and by *good* he means *pleasure*. He cannot make the meanings change places.

To say that what our deepest conscience calls darkness may be light to God is blasphemy. To say that light in God and light in man are of differing kinds is to speak against the spirit of light. God is light far beyond what we can see, but what we mean by light, God also means by light. What is light to God is light to us, or would be light to us if we saw it, and will be light to us when we do see it.

God means us to be jubilant in the fact that he is light—

that he is what his children, made in his image, mean when they say *light*. He wants us to rejoice that what we perceive as darkness in him only seems dark by excess of glory, by too much cause of jubilation. However dark it may be to our eyes, it is in fact light, and light as we mean it, light for our eyes and souls and hearts to take in the moment they are enough of eyes, enough of souls, enough of hearts, to receive it in its very being.

Living Light, thou wilt not have me believe anything dark of thee! Thou wilt have me so sure of thee as to dare to say that what I see as dark and unlike the Master cannot be of thee! If I am not honest enough, if the eye in me be not single enough to see thy light, thou wilt punish me, I thank thee, and purge my eyes from their darkness. Then they may be capable of letting the light in, and so shall I become an inheritor, with thy other children, of that light which is thy Godhead, and makes thy creatures need to worship thee. "In thy light we shall see light."

All men will not, in our present imperfection, see the same light. But light is light notwithstanding. And what each does see is his safety if he obeys it. In proportion as we have the image of Christ mirrored in us, we shall know what is and is not light. But never will anything prove to be light that is not of the same kind with that which we mean by light, with that in a thing which makes us call it light. The darkness yet left in us makes us sometimes doubt whether certain things be light or darkness. But when the eye is single, the whole body will be full of light.

AN EVER-ENLARGING ENOUGH

To fear the light is to be untrue, or at least it comes of untruth. No being needs fear the light of God, either for himself or another. Nothing in light can be hostile to our nature, which is of God, or inimical to anything in us that is worthy. All fear of the light, all dread lest there should be something dangerous in it, comes of the darkness still in those of us who do not love the truth with all our heart. It will vanish as we are more and more interpenetrated with the light.

In a word, there is no way of thought or action which we count admirable in man, in which God is not altogether adorable. There is no loveliness, nothing that makes man dear to his brother man that is not also in God, only it is infinitely better in God.

He is God our saviour. Jesus is our saviour because God is our saviour. He is the God of comfort and consolation. He will soothe and satisfy his children better than any mother her infant.

The only thing he will not give them is permission to stay in the dark—if a child cry, "I want the darkness," and complain that he will not give it, he will continue not to give it. He gives what his child *needs*—often by refusing what he *asks*.

If his child say, "I will not be good. I prefer to die—let me die!" his dealing with that child will be as if he said, "No. I have the right to make you content, not by giving you your own will but mine. That is your one good. You shall not die. You shall live to thank me that I would not hear your prayer.

You know what you ask, but not what you refuse."

There are good things God must delay giving until his child has a pocket to hold them—till he gets his child to make that pocket. He must first make him fit to receive and to have. There is no part of our nature that shall not be satisfied—and satisfied not by lessening it, but by enlarging it to embrace an ever-enlarging enough.

Come to God, then, my brother, my sister, with all your desires and instincts, all your lofty ideals, all your longing for purity and unselfishness, all your yearning to love and be true, all your aspirations after self-forgetfulness and child-life in the breath of the Father. Come to him with all your weaknesses, all your shames, all your futilities, all your helplessness over your own thoughts, all your failure, even with the sick sense of having missed the tide of true affairs. Come to him with all your doubts, fears, dishonesties, meannesses, paltrinesses, misjudgments, wearinesses, disappointments, and stalenesses. He will take you and all your miserable brood, whether of draggle-winged angels, or covert-seeking snakes, into his care—the angels for life, the snakes for death—and yourself for liberty into his limitless heart!

INTERPRETATIONS OF DARKNESS ARE THE WORK OF THE ENEMY

For he is light, and in him is no darkness at all. If he were a king, a governor, if the only name that described him were *The Almighty*, you might well doubt whether there could be light enough in him for you and your darkness. But he is your Father, and more your Father than the word can mean in any lips but his who said, "My father and your father, my God and your God."

And such a Father *is* light, an infinite, perfect light. If he were any less or any other than he is, and you could yet go on growing, you must at length come to the point where you would be dissatisfied with him. But he is light, and in him is no darkness at all.

If anything seems to be in him that you cannot be content with, be sure that the ripening of your love to your fellows and to him, the source of your being, will make you at length know that anything else than just what he is would have been to you an endless loss.

Do not be afraid to build upon the rock Christ, as if your holy imagination might build too high and heavy for that rock, thinking it will give way and crumble beneath the weight of your divine idea. Let no one persuade you that there is a little darkness in him because of something he has said which his creature interprets as darkness. The interpretation is the work of the enemy—a handful of tares of darkness sown in the light.

Neither let your cowardly conscience receive any word as light because another calls it light, while it looks to you dark. Say either that the thing is not what it seems or that God never said or did it.

Of all evils, to misinterpret what God does, and then say the thing as interpreted must be right because God does it, is of the devil. Do not try to believe anything that affects you as darkness. Even if you mistake and fail to see something true thereby, you will do less wrong to Christ by such an omission than you would by accepting as his what you can see only as darkness.

It is impossible you are seeing a true and real thing—seeing it as it is, I mean—if it looks to you darkness. But let your words be few, lest you say with your tongue what you will afterward repent with your heart.

Above all things *believe* in the light, that it is what you call light, though the darkness in you may give you occasional cause to doubt whether you are accurately seeing the light.

"But there is another side to the matter: God is light indeed, but darkness *does* exist. Darkness is death, and men are in it."

"Yes," I answer—"darkness is surely death, but not death to him that comes out of it."

It may sound paradoxical, but no man is condemned for anything he has done. He is condemned for continuing to do wrong. He is condemned for not coming out of the darkness, for not coming to the light, the living God, who sent the light, his son, into the world to guide him home.

GOD GIVES TIME

Let us hear what John says about the darkness.

For here also we have, I think, the word of the apostle himself. He begins at the thirteenth verse, I think, to speak in his own person. In the nineteenth verse he says, "And this is the condemnation"—not that men are sinners—not that they have done that which, even at the moment, they were ashamed of—not that they have committed murder, not that they have betrayed man or woman, not that they have ground the faces of the poor, making money by the groans of their fellows—not for any hideous thing are they condemned, *but that they will not leave such doings behind, and do them no more.*

This is the condemnation, that light is come into the world, and men would not come out of the darkness to the light, but "loved darkness rather than light, because their deeds were evil." Choosing evil, clinging to evil, loving the darkness because it fits with their deeds, therefore turning their backs on the in-breaking light. . . . If God be true, if he be light, and darkness be alien to him, how can they but be condemned? Whatever of honesty is in man, whatever of judgment is left in the world, must allow that their condemnation is in the very nature of things. It must rest on them, and remain so long as the conditions necessitating it remain.

But if one happens to speak some individual truth which another man has made into one of the cogs of his system, he is in danger of being supposed to accept all the toothed wheels and their relations in that system. I therefore go on to say that it does not follow, because light has come into the world, that it has fallen upon this or that man. He has his portion of the light that lighteth every man, but the revelation of God in Christ may not yet have reached him.

A man might see and pass the Lord in a crowd and not be

to blame, like the Jews of Jerusalem, for not knowing him. A man like Nathanael might have started and stopped at the merest glimpse of him, but all growing men are not yet like him without guile. Everyone who has not yet come to the light is not necessarily keeping his face turned away from it.

We dare not say that this or that man would not have come to the light had he seen it. We do not know that he will not come to the light the moment he does see it.

God gives every man time. There is a light that lightens sage and savage, but the glory of God in the face of Jesus may not have shined on this particular sage or that particular savage. The condemnation falls, rather, on those who, having seen Jesus, *refuse* to come to him, or *pretend* to come to him but *do not* the things he says. They have all sorts of excuses at hand. But as soon as a man begins to make excuse, the time has come when he might be doing that from which he excuses himself.

How many are there not who, believing there is something somewhere with the claim of light upon them, go on and on to get more out of the darkness! This consciousness, all neglected by them, gives broad ground for the expostulation of the Lord: *Ye will not come unto me that ye might have life!*

THAT WHICH CANNOT BE FORGIVEN

"All manner of sin and blasphemy," the Lord said, "shall be forgiven unto men; but the blasphemy against the spirit shall not be forgiven."

God speaks, as it were, in this manner: "I forgive you everything," he says. "Not a word more shall be said about your sins—only come out of them. Come out of the darkness of your exile. Come into the light of your home, of your birthright, and do evil no more. Lie no more, cheat no more, oppress no more, slander no more, envy no more, be neither greedy nor vain. Love your neighbour as I love you. Be my good child. Trust in your father. I am light—come to me and you shall see things as I see them, and hate the evil thing. I will make you love the thing which now you call good and love not. I forgive all the past."

"I thank thee, Lord, for forgiving me," some say, "but I prefer staying in the darkness. Forgive me that too."

"No," replies God, "that I cannot do. That is the one thing that cannot be forgiven—the sin of choosing to be evil and refusing deliverance. It is impossible to forgive that sin. It would be to take part in it. To side with wrong against right, with murder against life, cannot be forgiven. The thing that is past I pass. But he who goes on doing the same, annihilates this my forgiveness. He makes it of no effect. Let a man have committed any sin whatever, I forgive him. But to choose to *go on* sinning—how can I forgive that? It would be to nourish and cherish evil. It would be to let my creation go to ruin.

"Shall I keep you alive to do things hateful in the sight of all true men? If a man refuse to come out of his sin, he must suffer the vengeance of a love that would be no love if it left him there. Shall I allow my creature to be the thing my soul hates?"

THREE FORMS OF PUNISHMENT

There is no excuse for this refusal. If we were punished for every fault, there would be no end, no respite—we should have no quiet wherein to repent. But God passes by all he can. He passes by and forgets a thousand sins, yea, tens of thousands, forgiving them all—only we must begin to be good, begin to do evil no more.

He who refuses must be punished and punished—punished through all the ages—punished until he gives way, yields, and comes to the light, that his deeds may be seen by himself to be what they are, and be by himself reproved, and the Father at last have his child again. For the man who in this world resists to the full, there may be, perhaps, a whole age or era in the history of the universe during which his sin shall not be forgiven. But *never* can it be forgiven until he repents. How can they who will not repent be forgiven, except in the sense that God does and will do all he can to make them repent. Who knows but such sin may need for this cure the continuous punishment of an eon?

There are three conceivable kinds of punishment.

First, that of mere retribution, which I take to be entirely and only human. Therefore, indeed, it would more properly be called *inhuman*, for that which is not divine is not essential to humanity, and is of evil, and an intrusion upon the human.

Second, punishment which works repentance.

And finally, there is that punishment which refines and purifies, working for holiness. But the punishment that falls on those whom the Lord loves because they have repented is a very different thing from the punishment that falls on those whom he loves indeed but cannot forgive because they hold fast by their sins.

DIFFERENT FORMS OF FORGIVENESS

There are also various ways in which the word forgive can be used.

A man might say to his son: "My boy, I forgive you, but I must punish you, for you have done the same thing several times, and I must make you remember."

Or, again, he might say: "I am seriously angry with you. I cannot forgive you. I must punish you severely. The thing was too shameful! I cannot pass it by."

Or, once more, he might say: "Unless you alter your ways entirely, I shall have nothing more to do with you. You need not come to me. I will not take the responsibility of anything you do. So far from answering for you, I shall feel bound in honesty to warn my friends not to put confidence in you. Never, never, till I see a greater difference in you than I dare hope to see in this world, will I forgive you. I can no more regard you as one of the family. I would die to save you, but I cannot forgive you. There is nothing in you now on which to rest forgiveness. To say, I forgive you, would be to say, *Do anything you like, I do not care what you do.*"

So God may forgive and punish. And he may punish and not forgive, that he may rescue. To forgive the sin against the

Holy Spirit would be to damn the universe to the pit of lies, to render it impossible for a man so forgiven ever to be saved. He cannot forgive the man who will not come to the light because his deeds are evil. *We must become as little children.*

Insights Into
LIGHT

MICHAEL PHILLIPS

In many of his writings George MacDonald ploughs new
spiritual ground. In others he ploughs *old* ground that he
might plant *new* seeds.

His sermon entitled "Light," from *Unspoken Sermons,
Third Series*, is an example of the latter.

THE PLOUGH AND THE TELESCOPE

Ploughing old ground—hardened, perhaps frozen, un-
productive, compacted from years and prevented from being
penetrated by light—requires a sharp blade. Hard theologies
as well as fallow fields need occasionally to be upturned and

exposed to the light. When the time for such upturning comes, the plougher must courageously prepare his steel to bite deep. Only so can the broken earth be softened to receive the warmth of the sun.

George MacDonald's plough was his pen. And along with it he brought to his aid a more distant-seeing spiritual instrument to which we alluded earlier.

MacDonald's was truly a remarkable gift of communication. While exposing falsehood, he never allowed himself to be acrid for long. Once the furrow had been sliced through the hard-packed soil of orthodoxy and tradition, he then bid his readers look up to the sky with eyes and hearts open, there to receive truth and goodness from God's light.

At that point his imagination took over, giving wing to the intellectual foundations he had established. He did not attempt to define exactly in what form the light, the warmth, the breezes, the drifting clouds, and the blue of the heavens should speak their secrets. He merely pointed up with wonder in a hundred unique ways to say, "Behold . . . God is here!"

Most theological writings, and especially what might be called "studies" of various scriptural passages, are carried out with spiritual *microscopes,* shrinking and defining and categorizing and scrutinizing. MacDonald's writings are different. He instead places an imaginative *telescope* in our hands, then points above, that we might gaze into the distant heavens and there discover wonders about God and his ways unseen by the naked eye.

George MacDonald took courage from an intellect sharp-

ened and a heart softened by the influences of God's Fatherhood in his own life. Because of those influences, he was
single-minded and courageous to let his pen slice deep into
the Calvinist traditions that held so many Christians captive
to a false and hideous image of God, and then to let the telescope of his imagination peer toward the heavenly realms.

Thus are windows opened heavenward. But MacDonald
does not define and doctrinalize the view from the human end
of the telescope. He leaves the reader free to experience the
wonder of new revelation, in a sense, on his or her own terms.

TRUE GOSPEL AND FALSE GOSPEL

MacDonald first takes offense at what, in his opinion, is
wrongly called the "gospel."

> The so-called "deliverance" some think it brings might
> be founded on such notions of God as to not a few of us
> contain as little of good as of news. To share in the deliv-
> erance which some men find in what they call the gos-
> pel—for all do not apply the word to the tale itself, but
> to certain deductions made from the epistles . . . we
> should have to believe such things of God as would be the
> opposite of an evangel to us. Indeed, it would be a mes-
> sage from hell itself.

In order to bring "light" into the darkness of the frozen
ground of nineteenth-century Calvinist theology, MacDonald
begins this remarkable essay with a bold and astonishing accusation:

"You theologians," he says, "talk and preach about the good news. But you do not even know what the gospel is. Your so-called 'gospel' is *not* good news at all, and does not represent what the Lord came to bring."

Strong words.

His attack against what he considers a false theology of the gospel is as impassioned as the Lord's stinging indictment of first-century Pharisaism.

> To believe such things, we should have to imagine possibilities worse than any evil from which their "good news" might offer us deliverance. We would first have to believe in an unjust God from whom we have to seek refuge. True, he is called "just" by those holding to such theologies. But at the same time they say he does that which seems to the best in me the essence of *injustice.* . . .
>
> They make it a consequence of the purity and justice of God that he will judge us—born in evil, and for which birth we were not accountable—by our sinfulness instead of by our guilt.

If George MacDonald's single greatest outcry against false teaching could be identified, I think it likely is this:

That so many of those who call themselves Christians— especially their pastors, teachers, priests, and theologians— can be content to believe things of God (calling them attributes of "love") that, if they were said of any human being, would be uniformly set down as atrocities and cruelties unimaginable.

This he elsewhere calls a "duplicity in the church," an illogical blindness willing to attribute to God the most unloving, unjust, unmerciful, and illogical methods, and then, because "his ways are higher than our ways," to insist that those methods are founded in forgiveness, justice, mercy, and love.

He hated this duplicity, not merely for its falsehood against man, but also for its slander against the character of God.

MacDonald saw in such reasoning not mere falsehood and shallow thinking, but self-righteousness most foul, a contentment for God to act the part of an ogre who will condemn and torment souls of his own creation . . . if only the reasoners *themselves* are standing on the right side of the fiery pit.

> It may be "good news" to such as are content to have a God capable of unrighteousness, if only he be on *their* side!

From belief in such a God, MacDonald recoiled in horror. On numerous occasions in his writing does he affirm that he would rather be cast into the outer darkness himself, even to lose his God altogether, than to believe in the false God of man's twisted theologies.

Turning from these images, MacDonald succinctly affirms *true* gospel:

Jesus' "good news" about his Father is that he is no tyrant of men's fancies, but a loving, tender, and forgiving Father.

What in it makes it good news? . . .

It is the news Jesus brought concerning the Father . . . that God is light, and in him is no darkness at all.

Ah, my heart, this is indeed the good news! This is a gospel!

If God be light, what more, what else can I seek than God, than God himself! Away with your doctrines! Away with your salvation from the "justice" of a God whom it is a horror to imagine! Away with your iron cages of false metaphysics! I am saved—for God is light!

DARKNESS OF MAN, LIGHT OF GOD

MacDonald goes on to contrast the "darkness" of man's theologies with the light of the gospel. He adds that it is not necessary to understand all there is of God's light, only that we do not knowingly and willingly attribute to God what we know to be darkness.

Whatever seems to me darkness, that I will not believe of my God. If I should mistake . . . will he not reveal the matter to me? . . . Will he not break open the shell for me, and let the truth of it . . . stream out upon me?

He will not let it hurt me to mistake . . . as long as I do not . . . call darkness light. . . .

To say that what our deepest conscience calls darkness may be light to God is blasphemy. To say that light in God and light in man are of differing kinds is to speak against the spirit of light. God is light far beyond what we can

see, but what we mean by light, God also means by
light. . . .

He wants us to rejoice that what we perceive as darkness in him only seems dark by excess of glory, by too
much cause of jubilation.

As he continues, MacDonald addresses a timely difficulty,
amazingly relevant to our day as it obviously was to his.

What does one say to those trapped by years of allegiances
to what he calls the contorted theologies of men, the
traditions of the elders, doctrines that offer dreadful explanations of God's justice and love?

How does one respond to those afraid to venture beyond
the confines of such theologies, to those who consider it "dangerous doctrine" to be told that God is entirely and only full
of light?

How does one answer those who are afraid of *too* much
light, *too* much goodness, *too* much love attributed to the
Father of Jesus Christ?

If theirs is an honest fear, MacDonald says it will pass. For
darkness will always eventually give way to light. If it is a fear
based on love of untruth about God, then it reveals untruth
in the soul of him or who holds by it. To persist in clinging to
untruth is to set oneself contrary to God's purpose.

To fear the light is to be untrue. . . . All fear of the
light, all dread lest there should be something dangerous
in it, comes of the darkness still in those of us who do not
love the truth with all our heart. . . .

In a word, there is . . . no loveliness, nothing that

makes man dear to his brother man that is not also in God, only it is infinitely better in God.

He is God our saviour. Jesus is our saviour because God is our saviour. He is the God of comfort and consolation. He will soothe and satisfy his children better than any mother her infant.

The only thing he will not give them is permission to stay in the dark. . . . He gives what his child *needs*—often by refusing what he *asks*.

To believe dark falsehoods of God is to believe lies from the enemy.

Of all evils, to misinterpret what God does, and then say the thing as interpreted must be right because God does it, is of the devil. Do not try to believe anything that affects you as darkness. . . . It is impossible you are seeing a true and real thing—seeing it as it is, I mean—if it looks to you darkness. . . .

Above all things *believe* in the light. . . .

It may sound paradoxical, but no man is condemned for anything he has done. He is condemned for continuing to do wrong. He is condemned for not coming out of the darkness.

COME OUT OF THE DARKNESS

Then MacDonald redirects his emphasis. After challenging Christians who willingly believe darknesses about God, he turns his attention toward those whom Christ is calling, who may also, for much different reasons, refuse to come to the light of truth. In fact, the two *may* be the same—the falsehoods held by "believers," and the "unbelief" of unbelievers.

> God gives every man time. . . . The condemnation falls . . . on those who, having seen Jesus, *refuse* to come to him, or *pretend* to come to him but *do not* the things he says.

The focus now becomes evangelistic. One hears a reminder of MacDonald's character Thomas Wingfold in his fictional pulpit. Surely these words echo the heart's cry many listeners in many a pew heard from MacDonald's own lips in his time.

> God speaks, as it were, in this manner: "I forgive you everything," he says. "Not a word more shall be said about your sins—only come out of them. . . . Come into the light of . . . your birthright. . . . Lie no more, cheat no more, oppress no more, slander no more, envy no more, be neither greedy nor vain. Love your neighbour as I love you. Be my good child. Trust in your father. . . ."
>
> Come to God, then, my brother, my sister, with all your desires and instincts, all your lofty ideals, all your longing for purity . . . all your yearning to love . . . all your aspirations. . . . Come to him with all your weaknesses, all your shames, all your futilities . . . all your failure. . . . Come to him with all your doubts, fears, dishonesties, meannesses, paltrinesses, misjudgments, wearinesses, disappointments, and stalenesses. He will take you . . . into his care . . . into his limitless heart!

BLASPHEMY, PUNISHMENT, FORGIVENESS

I have wondered if this sermon might originally have ended with the words *Ye will not come unto me that you might have life!* What comes thereafter strikes me almost as a "coda" or "epilogue"—a brief essay on what is called the blasphemy against the Holy Spirit.

To be sure, the content of this conclusionary section is related in some measure to what has come before. But the flow and thematic tone feel distinct. To my ear, MacDonald shifts directions, and noticeably so. I am reluctant to question his chosen structure, yet in all honesty I cannot but think the final portion of this sermon was written at a different time.

The ideas presented in what follows are intriguing, and, more than that, what MacDonald has to say about the "blasphemy" against the Spirit and the three forms of punishment is extremely helpful. Yet I would prefer a separate essay on these additional important topics, especially in that the general theme of "light" he has been developing, to my literary sensibilities, is not satisfactorily concluded. Nevertheless, this is how the sermon comes to us from his pen.

Taking what we have before us, then, we discover a brilliant stroke of scriptural illumination concerning the passage that has troubled so many, that of the so-called "unforgivable sin" against the Holy Spirit. MacDonald says the unforgiveness is not a permanent judgment but instead represents a state or a condition, and, as such, that condition is subject to change. The unforgiveness lasts as long, and *only* as long, as the condition of *choosing* sin remains.

"I thank thee, Lord, for forgiving me," some say, "but I prefer staying in the darkness. Forgive me that too."

"No," replies God, "that I cannot do. That is the one thing that cannot be forgiven—the sin of . . . refusing deliverance. It is impossible to forgive that sin. It would be to take part in it. . . . The thing that is past I pass. But he who goes on doing the same, annihilates this my forgiveness. . . . Let a man have committed any sin whatever, I forgive him. But to choose to *go on* sinning—how can I forgive that?" . . .

God passes by all he can. He passes by and forgets a thousand sins, yea, tens of thousands, forgiving them all—only we must begin to be good, begin to do evil no more.

MacDonald's words on punishment are fascinating in light of what we know of his interest in the afterlife and the purposefulness of hell—he says elsewhere—as belonging to God, not the devil.

He who refuses must be punished . . . punished through all the ages—punished until he gives way, yields, and comes to the light. . . . For the man who in this world resists to the full, there may be, perhaps, a whole age or era in the history of the universe during which his sin shall not be forgiven. But *never* can it be forgiven until he repents. . . . Who knows but such sin may need for this cure the continuous punishment of an eon?

MacDonald then closes (again, abruptly), continuing briefly on the theme of punishment and adding a brief analogy of forgiveness. It is not exactly a summation of what has come before, yet is compelling in its own right.

There are three conceivable kinds of punishment.

First, that of mere retribution, which I take to be entirely and only human. . . .

Second, punishment which works repentance.

And finally, there is that punishment which refines and purifies, working for holiness. . . .

There are also various ways in which the word *forgive* can be used. . . .

God may forgive and punish. And he may punish and not forgive, that he may rescue. To forgive the sin against the Holy Spirit would be to damn the universe to the pit of lies, to render it impossible for a man so forgiven ever to be saved.

THE CHILD IN THE MIDST

GEORGE MACDONALD

*And he came to Capernaum: and, being in the house, he
asked them, What was it that ye disputed among yourselves
by the way? But they held their peace: for by the way they
had disputed among themselves who should be the greatest.*

*And he sat down, and called the twelve, and saith unto
them, If any man desire to be first, the same shall be last of
all, and servant of all. And he took a child, and set him in
the midst of them: and when he had taken him in his arms,
he said unto them, Whosoever shall receive one of such
children in my name, receiveth me: and whosoever shall
receive me, receiveth not me, but him that sent me.*

—MARK 9:33–37

Of this passage in the life of our Lord regarding the child, the account given by St. Mark is the more complete. But it may be enriched and its lesson rendered yet more evident from the record of St. Matthew:

> *Verily I say unto you, Except ye be converted, and become as little children, ye shall not enter into the kingdom of heaven. Whosoever shall humble himself as this little child, the same is greatest in the kingdom of heaven. And whoso shall receive one such little child in my name receiveth me. But whoso shall offend one of these little ones that believe in me, it were better for him that a millstone were hanged about his neck, and that he were drowned in the depth of the sea.*

These passages record a lesson our Lord gave his disciples against ambition and emulation. It is not for the sake of setting forth this particular lesson, however, that I write about these words of our Lord, as important as that lesson is. Instead, I write for the sake of a truth, a revelation about God himself. It is in that context that his great argument reaches its height.

THE LORD'S CHOICE OF A TYPE

Jesus took a little child—possibly a child of Peter. St. Mark says that the incident took place at Capernaum, and "in the house." Therefore, especially if Peter's, it might have been a child with some of the characteristics of Peter, whose very faults were those of a childish nature. We might expect the child of such a father to possess the childlike countenance and bearing essential for the lesson I believe the passage contains.

It must be pointed out that there are children who are not childlike. One of the saddest and not least common sights in the world is the face of a child whose mind is so full of worldly wisdom that the human *childishness* has vanished from it, as well as the divine *childlikeness*.

For the *childlike* is the divine. The very word sets me in the way I mean to go. But I must delay my ascent to the final argument in order first to remove a possible difficulty, which, in turning us toward one of the grandest truths, turns us away from the truth which the Lord had in view here.

The difficulty is this: Is it like the *Son of Man* to pick out the beautiful child and leave the common child unnoticed? What thanks would he have in that? Do not even the publicans as much as that? And do not our hearts revolt against the thought of it? Shall the mother's heart cleave closest to the deformed of her little ones, and shall "Christ as we believe him" choose the more pleasing to the sight of the eye?

Would he turn away from the child born in sin and taught iniquity, on whose pinched face hunger and courage and love of praise have combined to stamp the cunning of avaricious age, and take instead to his arms the child of honest parents, such as Peter and his wife—a child who could not help looking better than the other?

That could not be him who came to seek and to save that which was lost.

Let the man who loves his brother in his highest moments of love to God, when he is nearest to that ideal humanity whereby a man shall be a hiding-place from the wind, say which he would clasp to his bosom of refuge. Would it not be the evil-faced child, because he needed it most?

Yes—in God's name, yes. For is not that the divine way?

Who that has read of the lost sheep, or the prodigal, even if he had no spirit bearing witness with his spirit, will dare to say that it is not the divine way?

Often, no doubt, it will *appear* otherwise, for the childlike child is easier to save than the other, and may *come* first. But the rejoicing in heaven is greatest over the sheep that has wandered the farthest—perhaps was born on the wild hillside and not in the fold at all. For such a prodigal, the elder brother in heaven prays thus: *Lord, think about my poor brother more than about me, for I know thee, and am at rest in thee. I am with thee always.*

Why, then, do I think it necessary to say that this child was probably Peter's child, and certainly a child that looked childlike because it was childlike? No amount of evil can *be* the child. No amount of evil, not to say in the face, but in the habits, or even in the heart of the child, can make it cease to be a child. Nothing can annihilate the divine idea of childhood which moved in the heart of God when he made that child after his own image. It is the essential of which

God speaks, the real by which he judges, the undying of which he is the God.

Heartily I grant this. And if the object of our Lord in taking the child in his arms had been to teach love to our neighbour, love to humanity, the ugliest child he could have found would perhaps have served his purpose best. The man who receives any, and more plainly he who receives the repulsive child, because he is the offspring of God, because he is his own brother born, must receive the Father in thus receiving the child. Whosoever gives a cup of cold water to a little one refreshes the heart of the Father.

To do as God does is to receive God. To do a service to one of his children is to receive the Father. Hence, any human being, especially if wretched and woebegone and outcast, would do as well as a child for the purpose of setting forth this love of God to the human being.

Therefore something more is probably intended here. The lesson will be found to lie not in the *humanity* but in the *childhood* of the child.

THE LESSON OF ESSENTIAL CHILDHOOD

Again, if the disciples could have seen that the essential childhood was meant, and not a blurred and half-obliterated childhood, the most selfish child might have done as well, though perhaps no better, than one in whom true childhood is more evident. But when the child was employed as a manifestation and sign of the truth that lay in his childhood, in order that the eyes as well as the ears should be channels to the heart, it was essential that the child should be, not necessarily beautiful, but childlike. It was necessary that those qualities which wake in our hearts the love peculiarly belonging to childhood, which is, indeed, but the perception of the childhood, should at least glimmer out upon the face of the *chosen type*.

Would such an unchildlike child as we see sometimes, now in a great house clothed in purple and lace, now in a squalid alley clothed in dirt and rags, have been fit for our Lord's purpose, when he had to say that his listeners must become like this child—when the lesson he had to present to them was that of the divine nature of the child, that of *childlikeness*? Would there not have been a contrast between the child and our Lord's words, ludicrous except for its horror, especially seeing that he called attention to the individuality of the child by saying, "this little child . . . one of such children" and "these little ones that believe in me?" Even the feelings of pity and of love that would arise in a good heart upon further contemplation of such a child would have turned it quite away from the lesson our Lord intended to give.

That this lesson lay not in the humanity but in the *childhood of the child*, let me now show more fully.

The disciples had been disputing who should be the greatest, and the Lord wanted to show them that such a dispute had nothing whatever to do with the way things went in his kingdom. Therefore, as a specimen of his subjects, he took a child and set him before them.

It was not, it could not be, because of his humanity—it was in virtue of his *childhood* that this child was thus presented as representing a subject of the kingdom. It was not to show the scope but the *nature* of the kingdom. He told them they could not enter into the kingdom except by becoming little children—by humbling themselves.

The idea of ruling was excluded altogether where childlikeness was the one essential quality. Greatness in his kingdom would be known not by who should rule but who should serve. Such would no more look down upon its fellows from the conquered heights of authority—even of sacred authority—but would look up honouring humanity, and ministering unto it, so that humanity itself might at length be persuaded of its own honour as a temple of the living God.

It was to impress this lesson upon them that he showed them the child. Therefore, I repeat, the lesson lay in the *childhood* of the child.

But I now approach my specific object. For this lesson led to the enunciation of a yet higher truth upon which it was founded, and from which indeed it sprung. Nothing is required of man that is not first in God. It is because God is perfect that we are required to be perfect. And it is for the revelation of God to all the human souls, that they may be saved by knowing him, and so become like him, that this child is thus chosen and set before them in the gospel.

He who, in giving the cup of water or the embrace, comes into contact with the essential childhood of the child—that is, embraces the *childish* humanity of it (not he who embraces it out of love to humanity, or even love to God as the Father of it)—is partaker of the meaning and blessing of this passage. It is the recognition of the childhood as divine that will show the disciple how vain is the strife after relative place or honour in the great kingdom.

SPIRITUAL CHILDHOOD

For it is *in my name* that Jesus speaks of receiving the child.

This means *as representing me*, and, therefore, *as being like me*. Our Lord could not commission anyone to be received in his name who could not more or less represent him. To do so would involve untruth and unreason. Moreover, he had just been telling the disciples that they must become like this child. Now when he tells them to receive such a little child in his name, it must surely imply something in common between them all—something which meets in the child and in Jesus, and which meets in the child and the disciples.

What else could that be than the spiritual childhood?

In my name does not mean *because I will it*. An arbitrary utterance of the will of our Lord would certainly find ten thousand to obey it, even to suffering, for every one who will be able to receive such a vital truth of his character as is contained in the words. Yet it is not obedience alone that our Lord will have, but *obedience to the truth*, that is, to the Light of the World—truth beheld and known.

In my name, if we take all we can find in it—the full meaning which alone will harmonize and make the passage a whole—involves a revelation from *resemblance*, from fitness to represent and so reveal. He who receives a child "in the name of Jesus" does so by perceiving in what ways Jesus and the child are one, by recognizing what is common to them. He must not only see the *ideal* child in the child he receives—that reality of loveliness which constitutes true childhood—but must perceive that the child is like Jesus, or, rather, *that the Lord is like the child.* He may be embraced— indeed, he *is* embraced, by every heart childlike enough to embrace a child for the sake of his childness.

I do not therefore say that none but those who are con- scious of this truth in the act partake of the blessing. But a special sense, a lofty knowledge of blessedness, belongs to the act of embracing a child as the visible likeness of the Lord himself. For the blessedness is the perceiving of the truth— the blessing is the truth itself—the God-known truth, that the Lord has the heart of a child. The man who perceives this knows in himself that he is blessed—blessed because he has discovered the truth.

But the argument as to the meaning of our Lord's words, *in my name*, is incomplete until we follow our Lord's enunci- ation to its second and higher stage. "He that receiveth me receiveth him that sent me." It will be allowed that the con- nection between the first and second links of this chain will probably be the same as the connection between the second and third. I do not say it is necessarily so, for I aim at no logical certainty. I want to show rather than prove, by means of such sequences, the idea which I am approaching. For if, after beholding it, you cannot receive it, if it does not reveal itself to you as true, there would be little use in attempting to convince you by logic. But I admit that you might easily suggest other possible connections in the logical progressions, though, I assert, none so symmetrical.

What, then, is the connection between the second and third stages of the argument? How is it that one who receives the Son receives the Father? Because the Son is as the Father. He whose heart can perceive the essential in Christ has the essence of the Father—that is, he sees and holds to it by that recognition, and is therefore one by recognition and worship.

What, then, next, is the connection between the first and second stages? I think it is the same. "He that sees the essential in this child, the pure childhood, sees that which is the essence of me," grace and truth—in a word, childlikeness. It does not follow that the former is perfect as the latter, but it is the same in kind. Manifest in the child, it therefore reveals that which is in Jesus.

Then to receive a child in the name of Jesus is to receive Jesus. To receive Jesus is to receive God. Therefore to receive the child is to receive God himself.

The Nature of Christ's Kingdom

That such is the feeling of the words, and that such was the feeling in the heart of our Lord when he spoke them, I may show from another golden thread that may be traced through the shining web of his golden words.

What is the foundation of the kingdom of Christ?

It is based on a rule of love, of truth—a rule of *service*. The king is the chief servant in it:

"The kings of the earth have dominion: it shall not be so among you."

"The Son of Man came to minister."

"My Father worketh hitherto, and I work."

The great Workman is the great King, laboring for his own. So he that would be greatest among them, and come nearest to the King himself, must be the servant of all.

It is *like king, like subject* in the kingdom of heaven. No rule of force, as of one kind *over* another kind. It is the rule of *kind*, of *nature*, of deepest nature—of God.

If, then, to enter into this particular kingdom, we must become children, the *spirit of children* must be its pervading spirit throughout, from lowly subject to lowliest king.

The lesson added by St. Luke to the presentation of the child is: "For he that is least among you all, the same shall be great." And St. Matthew says: "Whosoever shall humble himself as this little child, the same is greatest in the kingdom of heaven."

Hence we see the sign that passes between king and subject. The subject kneels in homage to the kings of the earth. But the heavenly king takes his subject in his arms. This is the sign of the kingdom between them. This is the all-pervading relation of the kingdom.

To give one glance backward at this progression, then:

To receive the child because God receives it, or for its humanity, is one thing. To receive it because *it is like God,* or for its *childhood,* is another.

The former will do little to destroy ambition. Alone it might argue only a wider scope for ambition because it admits all men to the arena of the strife. But the latter strikes at the very root of emulation. The moment even service is done for the honour and not for the sake of service, the doer is that moment outside the kingdom. But when we receive the child in the name of Christ, the very childhood that we receive to our arms is humanity itself. We love its humanity in its childhood, for *childhood* is the deepest heart of humanity—its divine heart. And so in the name of the child we receive all humanity.

Therefore, although the lesson is not about humanity but about childhood, it returns upon our race, and we receive our race with wider arms and deeper heart. There is, then, no other lesson lost by receiving this as the primary lesson. There is no heartlessness in insisting that the child was a lovable, a childlike, child.

If there is in heaven a picture of this wonderful teaching, we shall no doubt see represented in it a dim childhood shining from the faces of all that group of disciples of which the centre is the Son of God with a child in his arms. The childhood, dim in the faces of the men, must be shining trustfully clear in the face of the child. But in the face of the Lord himself, the childhood will be triumphant—all his wisdom, all his truth upholding that radiant serenity of faith in his father.

Verily, O Lord, this childhood is life. Verily, O Lord, when thy tenderness shall have made the world great, then, children like thee, will all men smile in the face of the great God.

WHAT IS GOD THE FATHER LIKE?

And now we advance to the highest point of this teaching of our Lord: "He that receiveth me receiveth him that sent me."

To receive a child in the name of God is to receive *God himself*. How are we to receive him? In the only way he can be received—by knowing him as he is. To *know* him is to have him in us. And that we may know him, let us now receive this revelation of him, in the words of our Lord himself. Here is the argument of highest import founded upon the teaching of our Master in the utterance before us.

God is represented in Jesus, for God is *like* Jesus. In the same way, Jesus is represented in the child, for Jesus is *like* the child. Therefore, God is represented in the child, for he too is *like* the child.

God is childlike.

In the true vision of this fact lies the receiving of God in the child.

Having reached this point, there is little more to say about the argument. For if the Lord meant this as a truth, he that is able to receive it will receive it. He who has ears to hear it will hear it. Our Lord's arguments are for the presentation of the truth. The truth carries its own conviction to him who is able to receive it.

But the word of one such as myself who has seen this truth may help the dawn of a like perception in those who keep their faces turned toward the east and its aurora. For men may have eyes, and, seeing dimly, want to see more. Therefore let us reflect a little on the idea itself, and see whether it will not come forth so as to commend itself to that spirit, which, one with the human spirit where it dwells, searches the deep things of God. For, although the true heart may at first be shocked at the truth, as Peter was shocked when he said, "That be far from thee, Lord," yet will such a true heart, after a season, receive it and rejoice in it.

WHAT IS THE DIVINE NATURE?

Let me then ask: *Do you believe in the Incarnation?* And if you do, let me ask further: *Was Jesus ever less divine than God?*

I will answer for you: *Never.* He was lower, but never less divine.

Was he not a child then?

You answer, "Yes, but not like other children."

I ask, "Did he not look like other children?" If he *looked* like them and was not *like* them, then the whole thing was a deception, a masquerade at best.

I say that he was a child, whatever more he might be. God is man, and infinitely more. Our Lord became flesh, but did not *become* man. He took on him the form of man: he was man already. And he was, is, and ever shall be *divinely child-like*.

He could never have *been* a child if he would ever have *ceased* to be a child, for in him the transient found nothing. *Childhood belongs to the divine nature.*

Obedience, then, is as divine as *Will*, and *Service* is as divine as *Rule*.

How? Because they are one in their nature. They are both a doing of the truth. The love in them is the same.

The Fatherhood and the Sonship are one, except that the Fatherhood looks *down* lovingly, and the Sonship looks *up* lovingly.

Love is all. And God is all in all. He is ever seeking to get down to us—to be the divine man to us. And we are ever saying, "That be far from thee, Lord!"

We are careful, in our unbelief, over the divine dignity, of which he is too grand to think. Better pleasing to God, it needs little daring to say, is the audacity of Job, who, rushing into his presence, and flinging the door of his presence-chamber to the wall, like a troubled, it may be angry, but yet faithful, child, calls aloud in the ear of him whose perfect Fatherhood he has yet to learn: "Am I a sea or a whale, that thou settest a watch over me?"

LET US DARE BE BOLD TO DISCOVER GOD'S CHILDLIKENESS

Let us dare, then, climb the height of divine truth to which this saying of our Lord would lead us.

Does it not lead us to this: that the devotion of God to his creatures is perfect . . . that he does not think about himself but about them . . . that he wants nothing for himself but finds his blessedness in the outgoing of blessedness?

Ah! it is a terrible—shall it be a lonely glory this? We will draw near with our human response, our abandonment of self in the faith of Jesus. He gives himself to us—shall we not give ourselves to him? Shall we not give ourselves to each other whom he loves?

For when is the child the ideal child in our eyes and to our hearts? Is it not when with gentle hand he takes his father by the beard and turns that father's face up to his brothers and sisters to kiss? Is it not when even the lovely selfishness of love-seeking has vanished, and the heart is absorbed in loving?

In this, then, is God like the child: He is simply and altogether our friend, our Father—our more than friend, father, and mother—our infinite love-perfect God.

Grand and strong beyond all that human imagination can conceive of poet-thinking and kingly action, he is delicate beyond all that human tenderness can conceive of husband or wife, homely beyond all that human heart can conceive of father or mother. He does not have two opposing thoughts about us. With him all is simplicity of purpose and meaning and effort and end—namely, that we should be as he is, think the same thoughts, mean the same things, possess the same blessedness.

It is so plain that anyone may see it, every one ought to see it, everyone shall see it. It must be so. He is utterly true and good to us, nor shall anything withstand his will.

LET US DARE BE BOLD TO
KNOW THE FATHER OF JESUS

How terribly, then, have the theologians misrepresented God in the measure of the low and showy, not the lofty and simple humanities! Nearly all of them represent him as a great king on a grand throne, thinking how grand he is, and making it the business of his being and the end of his universe to keep up his glory, wielding the bolts of a Jupiter against them that take his name in vain.

They would not admit such a statement, but follow out what they say and it amounts to this.

Brothers, have you found our king? There he is, kissing little children and saying they are like God. There he is at the table with the head of a fisherman lying on his bosom, and somewhat heavy at heart that even he, the beloved disciple, cannot yet understand him well. The simplest peasant who loves his children and his sheep is—no, not a "truer," for the other is false, but—a *true* type of our God beside that monstrosity of a monarch that the theologians present.

Who is our God? It is he who is ever uttering himself in the changeful profusions of nature. It is he who takes millions of years to form a soul that shall understand him and be blessed. It is he who never needs to be, and never is, in haste. It is he who welcomes the simplest thought of truth or beauty as the return for seed he has sown upon the old fallows of eternity. It is he who rejoices in the response of a faltering moment to the age-long cry of his wisdom in the streets.

He is the God of music, of painting, of building, the Lord

of Hosts, the God of mountains and oceans. It is he whose laws go forth from one unseen point of wisdom, and thither return without an atom of loss. He is the God of history working in time unto Christianity.

And this our God is the God of little children! He alone can be perfectly, abandonedly simple and devoted.

The deepest, purest love of a woman has its well-spring in him. Our longing desires can no more exhaust the fullness of the treasures of the Godhead than our imagination can touch their measure. Of him not a thought, not a joy, not a hope of one of his creatures can pass unseen. And while one of them remains unsatisfied, he is not Lord over all.

Therefore, with angels and with archangels, with the spirits of the just made perfect, with the little children of the kingdom, yea, with the Lord himself, and for all them that know him not, we praise and magnify and laud his name in itself, saying, *Our Father*.

We do not draw back because we are unworthy, nor even because we are hardhearted and care not for the good. For it is his childlikeness that makes him our God and Father. The perfection of his relation to us swallows up all our imperfections, all our defects, all our evils. For our childhood is born of his fatherhood.

That man is perfect in faith who can come to God in the utter emptiness of feeling and desire, without a glow or an aspiration, with the weight of low thoughts, failures, neglects, and wandering forgetfulness, and say to him, "Thou art my refuge, because thou art my home."

Insights Into
THE CHILD
IN THE MIDST

MICHAEL PHILLIPS

A GLIMPSE INTO
GEORGE MACDONALD'S PRIORITY OF IDEAS

As noted previously, George MacDonald sometimes planted new seeds and sometimes ploughed completely new ground. If the preceding essay on light was the former, in "The Child in the Midst" he ploughs unheard-of new ground with the unbelievable claim that God is like a child.

Can you imagine the effect of his astonishing words in the ears of dour Scottish Calvinism: *God is like the child . . . it is his childlikeness that makes him our God and Father.*

Who else could conceive of God with the image of a child in his lap pulling at his beard!

It would be intriguing to know at what point during his lifetime MacDonald actually wrote the selections that went to comprise his volumes of *Unspoken Sermons*. The progression of ideas would make a fascinating study. Of one thing we can be certain: The fifty-some sermons he compiled for his five volumes of scriptural essays and studies represented topics and ideas he considered important to be addressed.

MacDonald preached and lectured on hundreds of occasions. Out of that vast wealth of material (does not the thought of an audio library of those addresses, in his wonderful Scottish tongue, make the heart leap!) he selected but these few to set down in permanent written form. "Unspoken" though he called them, one would imagine he certainly spoke on these topics through the thirty-five to forty years of his active public life, no doubt repeatedly. It is probably not too much to conjecture that in the pulpit he gradually honed and shaped the ideas for much of the wealth of these writings.

Given, however, that we are left to wonder about the progress of the ideas he emphasized, I find it captivating to reflect on the publication dates of his nonfiction. The contents, it seems to me, cannot be altogether accidental. The three volumes of *Unspoken Sermons* were published in 1867, 1885, and 1889. It strikes me that when MacDonald assembled the first of the three (originally entitled merely *Unspoken Sermons*) he could have had no way of knowing with certainty that more volumes would follow. This explains why there was

no "First Series" attached until much later printings. Therefore I am confident that he would naturally have included in
that first book what were to him, at the time, the most
important "sermons" he felt he had to deliver to his readers.
And indeed, it was not for eighteen years that a second volume appeared.

Among those first addresses, one stands at the top of the
list, so to speak. It represented the initial written sermon that
George MacDonald presented, and thus stands at the very
beginning of this new phase of his writing career—the very
first sermon from his pen that people would read.

That first among the first was *this* sermon: "The Child in
the Midst."

I think it no mere coincidence that it was chosen as the
first sermon in the first book of sermons. I believe George
MacDonald selected it to occupy this position of singular
honor in recognition of its significance in his eyes. This was, if
not at the apex of his priority of ideas, certainly close to it. If
people read nothing else in this book, he wanted to make sure
they were presented with this wonderful—though for some
shocking—perspective on the character and nature of God.

Nor is it only this first selection that deserves notice. It is
almost as if he set down in order the first three sermons of
Unspoken Sermons to mark out the theological foundations
upon which he would stake his reputation and establish his
career—three sermons that serve to define God's nature and
being, and the essence of faith itself. In each of the three
MacDonald makes a clear, bold statement concerning God's

character. He would enforce and amplify these ideas through-out the rest of his life.

How intriguing that the first three sermons, a new reader's introduction to George MacDonald as a theologian, were:

"The Child in the Midst," in which he wrote: *Our God is childlike.*

"The Consuming Fire," in which he wrote: *Our God is a consuming fire.*

"The Higher Faith," in which he wrote: *God is our Father.*

What a powerful trifecta upon which to build an image of God's fatherhood that would establish the basis for all that would follow from his pen in the ensuing thirty years!

THE CHILD JESUS SELECTED

MacDonald begins this particular study by making a most interesting distinction—between a self-centered and worldly child and a *childlike* child. His reason for doing so is to illuminate in the minds of his readers what he considers the essential lesson here to be gained, not the lesson against ambition or toward love for the unlovely (though, as he affirms, these are vital lessons, and ones the Lord *does* address elsewhere).

Rather, the operative lesson here is about God himself.

Thus MacDonald makes the distinction between the different potential "lessons" of the passage, concluding with his conviction that for the sake of this particular lesson, Jesus probably brought a child into their midst—possibly Peter's—whose countenance in its essence reflected the childlikeness to which he, the Lord, would point them.

When the child was employed as a manifestation and sign of the truth that lay in his childhood . . . it was essential that the child should be . . . childlike. It was necessary that those qualities which wake in our hearts the love peculiarly belonging to childhood . . . should at least glimmer out upon the face of the *chosen type*. . . . This lesson lay not in the humanity but in the *childhood of the child*. . . . It was in virtue of his *childhood* that this child was thus presented as representing a subject of the kingdom. It was not to show the scope but the *nature* of the kingdom.

THE CHILD'S COMMISSION

The lesson was simple—not that we are to love all humanity (as true and important as that injunction is), but that Jesus himself is childlike.

Nothing is required of man that is not first in God. It is because God is perfect that we are required to be perfect. . . .

He who . . . comes into contact with the essential childhood of the child . . . is partaker of the meaning and blessing of this passage. . . .

For it is *in my name* that Jesus speaks of receiving the child.

This means *as representing me*, and, therefore, *as being like me*. Our Lord could not commission anyone to be received in his name who could not more or less represent him.

Note MacDonald's use of the word *commission*. I find it an intriguing idea, worthy of his probing mind and childlike heart. In all the world, and out of all possible means open to him to communicate truth about his Father to the world, he says Jesus chose and *commissioned* a child to reveal to the world what he is like.

It is the one thing he has to teach concerning God's kingdom—spiritual childhood . . . true childness before the Father—and he commissions a child to help him teach it.

Why a child?

Because the child is like him. The child *resembles* from "fitness to represent and reveal."

> *In my name*, if we take all we can find in it . . . involves a revelation from *resemblance*. . . . He who receives a child "in the name of Jesus" does so by perceiving in what ways Jesus and the child are one . . . that the child is like Jesus, or rather, *that the Lord is like the child*.

Note too the distinction, an ever-present contrast in MacDonald, between the superficial *letter*—

> An arbitrary utterance of the will of our Lord would certainly find ten thousand to obey it.

—and the *spirit*, which points to God's character as the foundation of truth:

. . . for every one who will be able to receive such a vital truth of his character.

As he moves toward the highest stage of his progression, MacDonald emphasizes that a childlike spirit is the "pervading spirit" of God's kingdom for one reason alone: The child is like God himself.

> To receive a child in the name of Jesus is to receive Jesus. To receive Jesus is to receive God. Therefore to receive the child is to receive God himself. . . .
> It is *like king, like subject* in the kingdom of heaven. No rule of force, as of one kind *over* another kind. It is the rule of *kind*, of *nature*, of deepest nature—of *God*.
> If, then, to enter into this particular kingdom, we must become children, the *spirit of children* must be its pervading spirit throughout, from lowly subject to lowliest king. . . .
> To receive a child in the name of God is to receive *God himself*. . . .
> God is represented in Jesus, for God is *like* Jesus. In the same way, Jesus is represented in the child, for Jesus is *like* the child. Therefore, God is represented in the child, for he too is *like* the child.
> *God is childlike.*

BOLDNESS TO SEE GOD AS CHILDLIKE

MacDonald admits that the idea of God's childlikeness may be startling.

The true heart may at first be shocked at the truth, as Peter was shocked when he said, "That be far from thee, Lord," yet will such a true heart, after a season, receive it and rejoice in it.

But, he argues, can it be otherwise, since childlikeness is of the divine nature?

Let me then ask: *Do you believe in the Incarnation?* And if you do, let me ask further: *Was Jesus ever less divine than God?*

I will answer for you: *Never.* He was lower, but never less divine. . . .

Our Lord . . . was, is, and ever shall be *divinely childlike.* . . . *Childhood belongs to the divine nature.*

MacDonald then follows with a challenge: May we dare be bold enough to discover God in the child:

We are careful, in our unbelief, over the divine dignity, of which he is too grand to think. Better pleasing to God . . . is the audacity of Job, who, rushing into his presence, and flinging the door of his presence-chamber to the wall, like a troubled, it may be angry, but yet faithful, child, calls aloud in the ear of him whose perfect Fatherhood he has yet to learn. . . .

Let us dare, then, climb the height of divine truth. . . .

For when is the child the ideal child in our eyes and to our hearts? Is it not when with gentle hand he takes his father by the beard, and turns that father's face up to his brothers and sisters to kiss? . . .

In this, then, is God like the child: He is simply and

altogether our friend, our Father—our more than friend, father, and mother—our infinite love-perfect God. . . .

It is so plain that anyone may see it, every one ought to see it, everyone shall see it. It must be so. He is utterly true and good to us.

MacDonald concludes with one of the loftiest passages in all his writing, condemning theologies that wrongly character-ize God, then allowing his wonderfully poetic imagination to soar, offering a triumphant image of our God and Father.

How terribly, then, have the theologians misrepre-sented God. . . . Nearly all of them represent him as a great king on a grand throne, thinking how grand he is, and making it the business of his being and the end of his universe to keep up his glory, wielding the bolts of a Jupi-ter against them that take his name in vain. . . .

Brothers, have you found our king? There he is, kissing little children and saying they are like God. . . . The sim-plest peasant who loves his children and his sheep is . . . a *true* type of our God beside that monstrosity of a mon-arch that the theologians present.

Who is our God? It is he who is ever uttering himself in the changeful profusions of nature. It is he who takes millions of years to form a soul that shall understand him and be blessed. It is he who never needs to be, and never is, in haste. It is he who welcomes the simplest thought of truth or beauty as the return for seed he has sown upon the old fallows of eternity. . . .

He is the God of music, of painting, of building, the Lord of Hosts, the God of mountains and oceans. . . . He is the God of history working in time unto Christianity.

And this our God is the God of little children. . . .

Therefore, with angels and with archangels, with the spirits of the just made perfect, with the little children of the kingdom, yea, with the Lord himself, and for all them that know him not, we praise and magnify and laud his name in itself, saying *Our Father.* . . .

For it is his childlikeness that makes him our God and Father. . . . Our childhood is born of his fatherhood.

THE NEW NAME

GEORGE MACDONALD

To him that overcometh, I will give a white stone,
and in the stone a new name written,
which no man knoweth saving he that receiveth it.

—REVELATION 2:17

JOHN'S MYSTICAL MODE OF COMMUNICATION

Whether the book of the Revelation was written by the same man who wrote the gospel according to St. John or not, there is, at least, one element common to the two: the mysticism.

I use the word *mysticism* as representing a certain method of embodying truth, common, in various degrees, to almost all, if not all, the writers of the New Testament. The attempt to define it thoroughly would require an essay. I will hazard but one suggestion toward it. A mystical mind is one which, having perceived that the highest expression of which the truth admits lies in the symbolism of nature and the human customs that result from human necessities, prosecutes thought about truth so embodied by dealing with the symbols themselves after logical forms. This is the highest mode of conveying the deepest truth. The Lord himself often employed it. He did so, for instance, in the whole passage ending with the words, "If therefore the light that is in thee be darkness, how great is the darkness!"

The mysticism in the gospel of St. John is of the simplest and, therefore, noblest nature. No dweller in this planet can imagine a method of embodying truth that could be purer, loftier, or truer to the truth embodied. There may be higher modes in other worlds, or there may not—I cannot tell. But of all our modes these forms are the best illustrations of the highest. Apparently the mysticism of St. John's own nature enabled him to remember and report with sufficient accuracy the words of our Lord. His style has always seemed to me of a recognizably different kind from that of any of the writers of the New Testament—chiefly, perhaps, in the simplicity of its poetical mysticism.

But the mysticism in the book of the Revelation is more complicated, more gorgeous, less poetic, and occasionally, I think, perhaps arbitrary, or approaching the arbitrary. It *reminds* one of the mysticism of Emanuel Swedenborg. I will put aside both historical and literary criticism—in neither of which with regard to the authorship of these two books have I a right even to an opinion—and instead would venture to suggest that possibly the difference in tone between St. John's gospel and his revelation is just what one might expect when the historian of a mystical teacher and the recorder of his mystical sayings proceeds to embody his *own* thoughts, feelings, and inspiration—in other words, when the revelation flows no longer from the lips of the Master but through the disciple's own heart, soul, and brain. For surely not even the most idolatrous of our Bible-worshiping brothers and sisters will venture to assert that the Spirit of God could speak as freely by the lips of the wind-swayed, reed-like, rebukable Peter, or from the mouth of Thomas, who could believe his own eyes but neither the word of his brethren nor the nature of his Master, as by the lips of him who was blind and deaf to everything but the will of him that sent him.

Truth is truth, whether from the lips of Jesus or Balaam. But, in its deepest sense, *the truth* is a condition of heart, soul, mind, and strength toward God and toward our fellows. It is not an utterance, not even a *right* form of words. Therefore, such truth coming forth in words reveals, in a sense, the person that speaks. And many of the utterances of truth in the Revelation, commonly called of St. John, are not merely lofty in form but carry with them the conviction that the writer was no mere "trumpet of a prophecy," that he spoke of what he knew and testified of what he had seen.

In this passage quoted above about the gift of the white stone, I think we find the essence of spirituality.

THE IMAGE OF THE WHITE STONE

What notion was in the mind of the writer with regard to the white stone, I consider of comparatively little importance.

I take the stone to belong more to the arbitrary and imaginative than to the true mystical imagery, although for the bringing out of the mystical thought with which it is concerned, it is of high and honourable dignity. For fancy itself will subserve the true imagination of the mystic, and so be glorified.

I doubt if St. John himself associated any essential meaning with it. Certainly I will not allow that he had such a poor notion in it as that of a voting pebble—white, because the man who receives it is accepted or chosen. The word is used likewise for a precious stone set as a jewel. And the writer thought of it mystically, a mode far more likely to involve a reference to nature than to a political custom.

What his mystic meaning may be must be taken differently by different minds. I think he sees purity in its whiteness and indestructibility in its substance. But chiefly I regard the stone as the vehicle of the name—as the form in which the name is represented as passing from God to the man. What is involved in this communication is what I wish to show.

If my reader will not acknowledge my representation as St. John's meaning, I yet hope so to set it forth that he shall see the representation to be true in itself. Then I shall willingly leave the interpretation to its own fate.

WHAT IS EMBODIED IN A NAME?

In brief, I say that the giving of the white stone with the new name is the communication of what God thinks about a man to the man. It is the divine judgment, the solemn holy doom of the righteous man, the "Come, thou blessed," spoken to the individual.

In order to see this, we must first understand what is the idea of a name—that is, what is the perfect notion of a name. For, seeing that the mystical energy of a holy mind is here speaking of God as giving something, we must understand that *the essential thing* is intended, and not any of its accidents or imitations.

A name of the ordinary kind in this world has nothing essential in it. It is but a label by which one man and a scrap of his external history may be known from another man and a scrap of his history. The only names which have significance are those which popular judgment or prejudice or humour bestows, either for ridicule or honour, upon a few out of the many. Each of these is founded upon some external characteristic, upon some predominant peculiarity of temper, some excellence or the reverse of character, or something which he does or has done well or ill enough, or at least, singularly enough, to render him, in the eyes of the people, worthy of such distinction from other men. As far as they go, these are real names, for, in some poor measure, they express individuality.

The *true* name, however, is one which expresses the character, the nature, the being, the *meaning* of the person who bears it. It is the man's own symbol—his soul's picture, in a word—the sign which belongs to him and to no one else.

Who can give a man this, his own name?

God alone. For no one but God sees what the man is. No

one else, even if he could see what he is, could express in a name-word the sum and harmony of what he sees.

To whom are such names given? To those that overcometh. When are they given? When they have overcome.

Does God then not know what a man is going to become? As surely as he sees the oak which he put there lying in the heart of the acorn. Why then does he wait till the man has *become* by overcoming before he settles what his name shall be?

He does not wait. He knows his name from the first. But in the same way that repentance comes because God pardons, yet the man becomes aware of the pardon only in the repentance, so it is only when the man has *become* his name that God gives him the stone with the name upon it. For then first can he understand what his name signifies. It is the blossom, the perfection, the completion, that determines the name. God foresees that from the first because he made it so. But the tree of the soul, before its blossom comes, cannot understand what blossom it is to bear, and could not know what the word meant, which, in representing its own unarrived completeness, names itself.

Such a name cannot be given until the man *is* the name.

GOD'S IDEA OF THE MAN

God's name for an individual must then be the expression in a mystical word—a word of that language which all who have overcome understand—*of his own idea of the individual,* that being whom he had in his thought when he began to make the child, and whom he kept in his thought through the long process of creation that went to realize the idea.

To tell the name is to seal the success of that making—to say, "In thee also I am well pleased."

But we are still in the region of symbol. For supposing that such a form were actually observed between God and him that overcometh, it would be no less a symbol—only an acted one. We must therefore look deeper still for the fullness of its meaning.

Up to this point little has been said to justify our expectations of discovery in the text. Let us, I say, look deeper. We shall not look long before we find that the mystic symbol has for its centre of significance the fact of the personal individual relation of every man to his God. That every man has dealings and those his most important dealings, with God, stands to the reason of every man who associates any meaning or feeling with the words *Maker, Father, God.*

Even if we were but children for a day, with the understanding that someone had given us that one holiday, there would be something to be thought, to be felt, to be done, because we knew it. For then our nature would be according to our fate, and we could worship and die.

But it would be only the praise of the dead, not the praise of the living, for death would be the deepest, the lasting, the overcoming. We should have come out of nothingness, not of God. He could only be our Maker, not our Father, our Origin.

But we know that God *cannot* be the God of the dead— he must be the God of the living. To know that we died would freeze the heart of worship, and we could not say, *Our God*, or feel him worthy of such worth-ship as we could render.

To him who offers unto this God of the living his own self of sacrifice, to him that overcometh—one who has brought his individual life back to its source and who knows that he is *one* of God's children, *this* one of the Father's making—he gives the white stone. To him who climbs on the stair of all his God-born efforts and God-given victories up to the height of his being—that of looking face to face upon his ideal self in the bosom of the Father—God's *him*, realized in him through the Father's love in the Elder Brother's devotion—to him God gives the new name written.

GOD'S SECRET WITH EVERY INDIVIDUAL

But I leave this now, because that which follows embraces and intensifies this individuality of relation in a fuller development of the truth. For the name is one "which no man knows except he that receives it." Not only does each man and woman have his or her individual relation to God, but each has his *unique* relation to God.

He is to God a peculiar being, made after his own fashion, and that of no one else. For when he is perfected he shall receive the new name which no one else can understand.

Hence he can worship God as no other man or woman can worship him—can understand God as no one else can understand him. This or that individual may understand God more, may understand God better than another, but no other can understand God as he understands him.

God give me grace to be humble before you, my brother and sister, that I drag not my shadowy likeness of you before the judgment-seat of the unjust judge, but look up to yourself for what revelation of God you and no one else can give.

As the fir tree lifts up itself with a far different need from the need of the palm tree, so does each man stand before God and lift up a different humanity to the common Father. And for each God has a different response. With every man and woman he has a secret—the secret of the new name. In every individual there is a loneliness, an inner chamber of unique life into which only God can enter. I say not it is *the innermost chamber*—but a chamber into which no brother, nay, no sister can come.

From this it follows that there is a chamber also—

O God, humble and accept my speech!

—a chamber in God himself, into which none can enter but the one, the individual, the peculiar man. It is out of this chamber that man has to bring revelation and strength for his brethren. This is that for which he was made—to reveal the secret things of the Father.

By his creation, then, each man and woman is isolated with God. Each by his peculiar making, can say, *"My* God." Each can come to him alone and speak with him face to face as a man speaks with his friend. There is no *massing* of men with God. When he speaks of gathered men, it is as a spiritual *body*, not a *mass*. For in a body every smallest portion is individual, and therefore capable of forming a part of the body.

EACH OUR OWN
INDIVIDUAL FLOWER IN HIS GARDEN

Observe now what a significance the symbolism of our text assumes. Each of us is a distinct flower or tree in the spiritual garden of God—precious, each for our own sake, in the eyes of him who is even now making us. Each of us is watered and shone upon and filled with life for the sake of becoming his flower, his completed being, which will blossom out of us at last to the glory and pleasure of the great gardener.

Each of us has within us a secret of the Divinity. We are each growing toward the revelation of that secret to ourselves, and so to the full reception, according to his measure, of the divine.

Every moment that we are true to our true self, some new shine of the white stone breaks on our inward eye, some fresh channel is opened upward for the coming glory of the flower, the conscious offering of our whole being in beauty to the Maker.

Each individual, then, is in God's sight worthwhile. Life and action, thought and intent, are sacred.

And what an end lies before us!

To have a consciousness of our own ideal being flashed into us from the thought of God!

Surely this may well give way all our paltry self-consciousnesses, our self-admirations, and self-worships! Surely to know what he thinks about us will pale out of our souls all our thoughts about ourselves!

We may well hold them loosely now, and be ready to let them go. Toward this result St. Paul had already drawn near when he who had begun the race with a bitter cry for deliverance from the body of his death was able to say that he judged his own self no longer.

ENDLESS ASPIRATION IN THE DEATH OF AMBITION

"But," do some object, "is there not the worst of all dangers involved in such teaching—the danger of spiritual pride?"

If there be, are we to refuse the Spirit for fear of the pride? Or is there any other deliverance from pride except the Spirit? Pride springs from supposed success in the high aim: With attainment itself comes humility. But here there is no room for ambition. Ambition is the desire to be above one's neighbour, but here there is no possibility of comparison with one's neighbour. No one knows what the white stone contains except the individual who receives it.

Here there is room for endless *aspiration* toward the unseen ideal, but none for *ambition*. Ambition would only be higher than others, while aspiration would simply be high.

Relative worth is not only unknown—to the children of the kingdom it is unknowable. Each esteems the other better than himself. How shall the rose, the glowing heart of the summer heat, rejoice because it is compared against the snowdrop risen with hanging head from the white bosom of the snow? *Both* are God's thoughts. Both are dear to him. Both are needful to the completeness of his earth and the revelation of himself.

"God has cared to make me for himself," says the victor with the white stone, "and has called me that which I like best. For my own name must be what I would have it, seeing it is myself. What does it matter whether I be called a grass of the field, or an eagle of the air, a stone to build into his temple, or a Boanerges to wield his thunder? I am his. I am his idea, his making. I am perfect in my kind, yea, perfect in his sight. I am full of him, revealing him, alone with him. Let him call me what he will. The name shall be precious as my life. I seek no more."

Gone then will be all anxiety as to what one's neighbour may think about him. It is enough that God thinks about him. To be something to God—is not that praise enough? To be a thing that God cares for and would have complete for himself, because it is worth caring for—is not that life enough?

EACH A PROPHET

In such knowing, none will thus be isolated from his fellows. For what we say of one, we will say of all. It is as *one* that each has claims amongst his fellows. Each will feel the sacredness and awe of his neighbour's dark and silent speech with his God. Each will regard the other as a prophet, and look to him for what the Lord hath spoken. Each, as a high priest returning from his Holy of Holies, will bring from his communion some glad tidings, some gospel of truth, which, when spoken, his neighbours shall receive and understand. Each will behold in the other a marvel of revelation, a present son or daughter of the Most High, come forth from him to reveal him afresh. In God, each will draw nigh to each.

Yes, there will be danger—danger as everywhere. But he gives more grace. And if the man who has striven up the heights should yet fall from them into the deeps, is there not that fire of God to save him, the consuming fire, which burns and destroys not?

To no one who has not already had some speech with God, or who has not at least felt some aspiration toward the fount of his being, can all this appear other than foolishness. So be it.

But, Lord, help them and us, and make our being grow into thy likeness. Though it take ages of strife and ages of growth, yet let us at last see thy face, and receive the white stone from thy hand. That thus we may grow, give us day by day our daily bread. Fill us with the words that proceed out of thy mouth. Help us to know the truth, because we know you and believe the truth you have spoken to us.

Insights Into

THE NEW NAME

MICHAEL PHILLIPS

WHO GIVES A TRUE NAME?

I have two friends (curiously, of diametrically opposite spiritual persuasion), each of whom some twenty-five years ago changed his name to what each perceived as a more real expression of *true* identity and, in one case, spiritual and prophetic destiny.

I found the thing perplexing then . . . and it seems all the more so to me now. The particularly spiritually minded of my friends has not fulfilled the prophetic label to which he has all these years aspired. It strikes me as an example of our getting in God's way (do not each of our lives contain more such than we want to remember!)—of horning in on God's domain rather than waiting for *him* to do what he purposes. I have not changed my name, but I have blocked God's deeper purpose in my life many times by getting the cart of my ambitions ahead of the horse of his timing.

Now, in one sense my two friends perceived a great truth, that the "names" by which we are all known represent but a "label by which one man and a scrap of his external history may be known from another man and a scrap of his history." But as MacDonald adds, there is "nothing essential in it." My friends grasped a high truth, that our external *names* do not necessarily accurately reflect who we really *are* in the depths of our being.

Yet who can know who we truly are?

We ourselves are probably the least capable of knowing it. As long as we are *becoming,* how should we see what lies at the end of that process? Indeed, how can any person see what God purposes to make of him given enough time and enough cooperation on the person's side against the lower part of his nature?

Only the one who created us can know who we *are.* He can know because he knows who and what we are *becoming,* who and what we are meant for, who and what he envisioned us to be in the perfection of his mind's eye when he created us. He knows because he is both the *Originator* and the *Become-or,* the active force that Fathered us into being, and the nurturing force that is helping us, propelling us, urging us, goading us, inviting us, compelling us to *become* all that we will and shall become.

He only can see into every aspect of this becoming process, from the moment we were conceived till we shall arrive at the glorified perfection toward which he is leading us. Who but our Father should know the *name* (to use our own limited terminology for the high thing which cannot be embodied in a single word of humanity) into which the fullness of that becoming shall be embodied?

THE PERSONAL INDIVIDUAL RELATION OF EVERY MAN TO HIS GOD

So indeed, we all possess another name, a name already in formation, a name that is God's name for us, the name in which and through which he purposes for us to fulfill our eternal destiny. Each of us will rise into that destiny as his unique and uniquely named child. It is not a "name" merely. The new name God shall give us comprises the completeness of essential being.

When will he give it?

He has already given it, given it in possibility and potentiality. *He* already calls us by our true name in his heart. But we must grow into readiness to receive it from his heart . . . when we have overcome.

He looks at the acorn and thinks *oak*. But the acorn does not yet know what God is thinking.

So with us. Like the acorn, our duty is not to try to discern the name before its time. To us is given the responsibility to send down roots and grow and become strong by obeying that to which we have been called. Then one day we shall become capable of recognizing what God has been calling us all along. When he calls our name, we will then be ready to answer.

"The New Name" (like several of the selections in this compilation, from *Unspoken Sermons, First Series*) truly represents one of George MacDonald's remarkable written expressions of insight into the intimacy between God the Father and his "overcoming" sons and daughters. Of the extreme importance of the ideas here contained, we get some idea by his statement: "In this passage . . . about the gift of the white stone, I think we find the essence of spirituality."

MacDonald speaks often of that Father-child relationship. But here he probes deeply into the mechanism of that "lonely bond"—that place where only God knows the deepest regions of the heart.

> Not only does each man and woman have his or her individual relation to God, but each has his *unique* relation to God.
>
> He is to God a peculiar being, made after his own fashion, and . . . when he is perfected he shall receive the new name which no one else can understand. . . .
>
> With every man and woman he has a secret—the secret of the new name. In every individual there is a loneliness, an inner chamber of unique life into which only God can enter.

At the same time, he explores that unique place in God's heart where only I, and no one else, can go.

What a far-reaching idea!

MacDonald continually deepens our awareness of what true intimacy with the Father means. Even as he does he seems aware of what a staggering notion it is, and of his own capacity to put it into words at all.

> From this it follows that there is a chamber also—
> O God, humble and accept my speech!
> —a chamber in God himself, into which none can enter but the one, the individual, the peculiar man. . . . This is that for which he was made. . . .
> By his creation, then, each man and woman is isolated with God.

Here is intimacy indeed—that we may come and go in constant exchange with God, between our heart and his. He is free to enter ours where no one else goes, and we are free to probe reaches within the Godhead that are ours alone. Can there be a more intimate *knowing* than this?

> Each of us is a distinct flower or tree in the spiritual garden of God—precious, each for our own sake, in the eyes of him who is even now making us. Each of us is watered and shone upon and filled with life, for the sake of becoming his flower, his completed being, which will blossom out of us at last to the glory and pleasure of the great gardener.

Lonely, MacDonald calls it. But a divine loneliness!

For the Lord knows our *true* name, that which we have always been and that which we were meant for, that which we shall become when the fullness of our new name is revealed. We shall become it because we are becoming it even now.

TO OVERCOME

As to whom such names are given:

To those that overcometh. When are they given? When they have overcome.

Does God then not know what a man is going to become? As surely as he sees the oak which he put there lying in the heart of the acorn. . . . He knows his name from the first. But . . . it is only when the man has *become* his name that God gives him the stone with the name upon it. For then first can he understand what his name signifies. It is the blossom, the perfection, the completion, that determines the name. God foresees that from the first because he made it so.

What then is it to "overcome"?

The very word will conjure up notions of certain theologies prevalent in our time. We must do our best to leave these images, however, for MacDonald's use is entirely different.

What is to be overcome?

Obviously, sin.

What kind of sin?

Sin in our own lives. Anything contrary to the will of God, anything that prevents our saying, *Not my will, but yours be done*. Anything that prevents our being God's obedient sons and daughters.

To understand MacDonald's use of *overcome*, we return to one of his signature tunes, the free relinquishment of the human will to will its own.

We are God's children. We must learn to become his sons and daughters. We become his sons and daughters by bringing back to him the very free will he gave us, offering it as the sacrifice of a new and higher childship. As long as we cling to our own wills, we are mere children. Rising to become his sons and daughters, we say, "You gave me power to will. I now choose as an act of that will to lay down my will and take your will for my own."

This act of freely chosen childship MacDonald elsewhere calls the "creation" in Christ—the freely chosen relinquishment of self-will.

This relinquishment of self-will MacDonald here calls "overcoming." It is not overcoming of sin by brute force, but instead by the laying down of self-will (and with it the *desire* to sin) into God's will. By such overcoming relinquishment do we enter into the region where at last we become true sons and daughters.

Thus do we prove ready to inherit the new name.

To him who offers . . . his individual life back to its source and who knows that he is *one* of God's children . . . he gives the white stone. . . .

Each of us has within us a secret of the Divinity. We are each growing toward the revelation of that secret to ourselves, and so to the full reception, according to his measure, of the divine.

Every moment that we are true to our true self, some new shine of the white stone breaks on our inward eye, some fresh channel is opened upward for the coming glory of the flower, the conscious offering of our whole being in beauty to the Maker.

I am struck again with the quiet depth and profound implications of this amazing sermon. It cannot be "analyzed" in any accurate sense of the word. We simply must let its profound truth flow over us and gently sink into our spirits.

It is with a certain trepidation, as though I am intruding on hallowed ground, that I have added these few thoughts of my own. May they stumble no one, perhaps here and there shining a feeble light along the path.

May we all, at the end of the day, simply read this selection over again, slowly and in the quietness of our own secret chambers with God, and ask him to reveal his truth to us through the words of this remarkable man who knew the Father's heart.

THE KNOWING OF THE SON

GEORGE MACDONALD

Ye have neither heard his voice at any time, nor seen his shape. And ye have not his word abiding in you; for whom he hath sent, him ye believe not.

—JOHN 5:37–38

HOW ACCURATE ARE THE PRECISE GREEK WORDS?

One day we shall know just how near we come in the New Testament to the actual words of the Lord. That we have them different than he actually spoke them, I cannot doubt. For one thing, I do not believe he spoke in Greek. He was sent to the lost sheep of the house of Israel and would speak their natural language. He would not use a speech which, at best, they knew in secondary fashion. I cannot think that the thoughts of God would come out of the heart of Jesus in anything but the mother-tongue of the simple men to whom he spoke. He may perhaps have spoken to the Jews of Jerusalem in Greek, for they were less simple. But at present I do not see ground to believe he did.

Even further, I inquire: Are we bound to believe that John Boanerges, who indeed best, and in some things alone, understood him, after such a lapse of years was able to give us in his gospel, supposing the Lord to have spoken to his disciples in Greek, the *very* words in which he uttered the simplest profundities ever heard in the human world? I do not say John could not have done so. I only ask if we *must* believe that he did.

When the disciples became, by the divine presence in their hearts, capable of understanding the Lord, they remembered things he had said which they had forgotten. Possibly the very words in which he said them returned to their memories. But must we believe the evangelists always precisely recorded his exact words?

The little differences between their accounts is answer enough. The gospel of John is the outcome of years and years of remembering, recalling, and pondering the words of the Master, one thing understood recalling another. We cannot tell how much the memory, in its best condition—that is, with God in the man—may not be capable. But I do not believe that John would have always given us the very words of the Lord, even if, as I do not think he did, he had spoken them in Greek.

God has not cared that we should anywhere have assurance of his precise words. The reason is not merely because of the tendency in his children toward word-worship, false logic, and corruption of the truth. It is also because he would not have them oppressed by words. Being human, words are but partially capable, and could not absolutely contain or express what the Lord meant. To be understood, even he must depend upon the spirit of his disciple. Seeing it could not give life, the letter should not be throned with power to kill. It should be but the handmaid to open the door of the truth to the mind that is *of* the truth.

A RIGHT SPIRIT IS REQUIRED FOR UNDERSTANDING

"Then you believe in an individual inspiration to anyone who chooses to lay claim to it?"

Yes, to everyone who claims it from God; not to everyone who claims from men the *recognition* of his possessing it. He who has a thing does not need to have it recognized. If I did not believe in a special inspiration to every man who asks for the Holy Spirit, the good thing of God, I should have to throw aside the whole tale as an imposture. For according to that story, the Lord has promised such inspiration to those who ask for it. If an objector does not have this spirit, and is not inspired with the truth, he knows nothing of the words that are spirit and life. His objection is less worth heeding than that of a savage to the assertion of a chemist. His assent equally is but the blowing of an idle horn.

"But how is one to tell whether it be in truth the Spirit of God that is speaking in a man?"

You are not called upon to tell. The question for you is whether you have the Spirit of Christ *yourself*. The question is for you to put to yourself, the question is for you to answer to yourself: *Am I alive with the life of Christ? Is his spirit dwelling in me?*

Everyone who desires to follow the Master has the spirit of the Master, and will receive more, that he may follow closer, nearer, in his very footsteps. He is not called upon to prove to this or that or any man that he has the light of Jesus. He has to let his light shine.

It does not follow that his work is to teach others, or that he is able to speak large truths in true forms. When the strength or the joy or the pity of the truth urges him, let him speak it out and not be afraid—content to be condemned for it. Let him be comforted that if he mistake, the Lord himself will correct him, and save him "as by fire." The condemnation of his fellowmen will not hurt him, nor a whit the more that it be spoken in the name of Christ. If he speak true, the Lord will say, "I sent him." For all truth is of him. No man can see that a thing is true but by the Lord, the Spirit.

"How am I to know that a thing is true?"

By *doing* what you know to be true. By calling nothing true until you see it to be true. By shutting your mouth until the truth opens it. Are you meant to be silent? Then woe to you if you speak.

MISTAKE WILL NOT HURT,
BUT HYPOCRISY IS BLINDNESS

"But if I do not take the words attributed to him by the evangelists for the certain, absolute, very words·of the Master, how am I to know that they represent his truth?"

By seeing in them what corresponds to the plainest truth he speaks and commends itself to the power that is working in you to make of you a true man or woman. By their appeal to your power of judging what is true. By their rousing of your conscience. If they do not seem to you true, either they are not the words of the Master, or you are not yet true enough to understand them.

Be certain of this, that if any words that are his do not show their truth to you, then you have not received his message in them—they are not yet the word of God to you. They have not yet become spirit and life in you. They may be the nearest to the truth that words can come. They may have served to bring many into contact with the heart of God. But for *you* they remain as yet hidden. If your heart is true, it will revere them because of the probability that they are words with the meaning of the Master behind them. They will be to you as the rock in the desert before Moses spoke to it.

If you wait, your ignorance as to their meaning will not hurt you. If you presume to reason prematurely from them, you are a blind man disputing about that which you are not able to see. To reason from a thing you do not understand is to walk straight into the mire. To dare to reason about truth from words that do not show to us that they are true is the presumption of Pharisaical hypocrisy. Only they who are not true are capable of doing so.

Humble mistakes will not hurt us. The truth is there, and the Lord will see that we come to know it. We may think we know it when we have scarce a glimpse of it. But the error of a true heart will not be allowed to ruin it. Certainly that heart would not have mistaken the truth except for the untruth yet remaining in it. But he who casts out devils will cast out that devil.

In the passage under consideration, I see enough to enable me to believe that its words embody the mind of Christ. If I could not say this, I should say, "The apostle has here put on record a saying of Christ's, but I have not yet been able to recognize the mind of Christ in it. Therefore I conclude that I do not yet understand it, for to understand what is true is to know it true."

I have yet seen no words credibly reported as the words of Jesus concerning which I dared to say, "His mind is not therein, therefore the words are not his." The mind of man can receive any word only in proportion as it is the word of Christ, and in proportion as he is one with Christ. To him who does receive his word in this way, it is a power, not of argument, but of life. The words of the Lord are not for the logic that deals with words as if they were things, but for the spiritual logic that reasons from divine thought to divine thought, dealing with spiritual facts.

THE DEEPER MEANING OF WORDS AND CREATION

No thought, human or divine, can be conveyed from man to man except through the symbolism of the creation. The heavens and the earth are around us that it may be possible for us to speak of the unseen by the seen. For the outermost husk of creation has correspondence with the deepest things of the Creator. He is not a God that hides himself but a God who *made* that he might *reveal*. He is consistent and one throughout.

There are things with which an enemy hath meddled. But there are more things with which no enemy can meddle, and by which we may speak of God. They may not have revealed him fully to us, but at least when he *is* revealed, they will show themselves so much of his nature that we will at once recognize and use them as spiritual tokens in the commerce of the Spirit, to help convey to other minds what we may have seen of the unseen. The words of the Lord which I would now look into belong to this sort of mediation.

"And the Father himself which hath sent me hath borne witness of me. Ye have neither heard his voice at any time, nor seen his shape. And ye have not his word abiding in you: for whom he hath sent, him ye believe not."

If Jesus said these precise words, he meant more, not less, than lies on their surface. They cannot be mere assertion of what everybody already knew. Neither can their repetition of similar negations be but the saying over of the same thing in different words. They were not intended to inform the Jews of a fact they would not have dreamed of denying. Who among them would say he had ever heard God's voice or seen his shape? John himself says, "No man hath seen God at any time."

So we must ask, what is the *tone* of the passage?

It is one of reproach. Would Jesus then reproach them for not seeing God when no one has ever seen God, and when Paul says that no one man *can* see him?

Is there a paradox here? There cannot be the false argument: "No man hath seen God; ye are to blame that ye have not seen God; therefore all men are to blame that they have not seen God!"

If we read it instead as "No man hath seen God, but some men ought to have seen him," we do not therein find such hope for the race as will give the aspect of a revelation to the assurance that not one of those capable of seeing him has ever seen him!

So why did Jesus reproach them for not seeing?

The answer is found by recognizing that the one statement is from John, the other from his Master. If there is any contradiction between the two, of course the words of John must be thrown away. But there can hardly be a contradiction, since he who says the one thing is the recorder of the other as said by his Master, him to whom he belonged, whose disciple he was, whom he loved as never man loved man before.

SEEING AND SEEING

The word *see* is used in one sense in the one statement, and in another sense in the other. In the one it means *see with the eyes*. In the other, *with the soul*. The one statement is made about all men, the other is made to certain of the Jews of Jerusalem concerning themselves. It is true that no man has seen God, and true that some men ought to have seen him. No man has seen him with his *bodily* eyes; these Jews ought to have seen him with their *spiritual* eyes.

No man has ever seen God in any outward, visible, close-fitting form of his own. He is revealed in no shape except that of his Son. But multitudes of men have with their *mind's*—or rather their *heart's*—eye, seen more or less of God. And perhaps every man *might have* and *ought to have* seen something of him. We cannot follow God into his infinitesimal intensities of spiritual operation any more than into the atomic life-potencies that lie deep beyond the eye of the microscope. Similarly, God may be working in the heart of a savage in a way that no wisdom of his wisest, humblest child can see, or imagine that it sees. Many who have never beheld the face of God may yet have seen the vastness of his shadow. Thousands who have never felt the warmth of its folds have yet been startled by

No face: only the sight
Of a sweepy garment vast and white.

Some have dreamed his hand laid upon them who never knew themselves gathered to his bosom. The reproach in the words of the Lord is the reproach of men who *ought* to have had an experience they had not had.

Let us look a little closer at his words.

"Ye have not heard his voice at any time" might mean, *Ye have never listened to his voice,* or *Ye have never obeyed his voice.*

But the phrase "nor seen his shape" keeps us rather to the

primary sense of the word *hear*: The sound of his voice is unknown to you. You have never heard his voice so as to know it for his.

"You have not seen his shape": *You do not know what he is like.*

Plainly he implies, *You ought to know his voice. You ought to know what he is like.*

"You have not his word abiding in you." *The word that is in you from the beginning, the word of God in your conscience, you have not kept with you, it is not dwelling in you. By yourselves accepted as the witness of Moses, the Scripture in which you think you have eternal life does not abide with you. It is not at home in you. It comes to you and goes from you. You hear, heed not, and forget. You do not dwell with it, and brood upon it, and obey it. It finds no acquaintance in you. You are not of its kind. You are not of those to whom the word of God comes. Their ears are ready to hear. They hunger after the word of the Father.*

THE SOURCE OF THEIR UNSEEING

On what does the Lord base this accusation of them? What is the sign of their ignorance of God? "For whom he hath sent, him ye believe not."

"How so?" the Jews might answer. "Have we not asked from you a sign from heaven, and have you not point-blank refused it?"

The argument of the Lord was indeed of small weight

with, and of little use to, those to whom it most applied. For the more it applied, the more incapable they were of seeing that it did apply. But his words would be of great force upon some who stood listening, for their minds were more or less open to the truth, and their hearts were drawn to the man before them.

His argument was this:

"If you had ever heard the Father's voice, if you had ever known his call, if you had ever imagined him, or a God anything like him, if you had cared for his will so that his word was at home in your hearts, then you would have known me when you saw me. You would have known that I must come from him and that I must be his messenger. Thus, you would have listened to me.

"The least acquaintance with God, such as any true heart must have, would have made you recognize that I came from God. By the light of his word abiding in you, by his shape that you had beheld, however vaguely, in me, and by the likeness of my face and my voice to those of my Father, you would have been capable of knowing me. You would have seen my Father in me. You would have known me by the little you knew of him. The family-feeling would have been awake in you, the holy instinct of the same spirit, making you know your elder brother.

"That you do *not* know me now, as I stand here speaking to you, is because you do not know your own Father, even my Father. Throughout your lives you have refused to do his will and therefore have not heard his voice. You have shut your eyes from seeing him and have thought of him only as a partisan of your ambitions. If you had loved my Father, you would have known his Son."

And I think he might have also added, "If even you had loved your neighbour, you would have known me, for I am neighbour to the deepest and best in you."

WHAT WOULD HE LOOK LIKE TODAY?

If the Lord were to appear this day in England as he once did in Palestine, he would not come in the halo of the painters, or with that wintry shine of effeminate beauty and sweet weakness in which it is their helpless custom to represent him. Neither would he probably come as a carpenter, mason, or gardener. He would come in such form and condition as might bear to the present England, Scotland, and Ireland, a relation like that which the form and condition he then came in bore to the motley Judea, Samaria, and Galilee.

If he came thus, in a form altogether unlooked for, who would they be who would recognize and receive him?

The idea involves no absurdity. If the old story be indeed more than the best and strongest of the fables that possess the world, he is near us every moment. He might at any moment appear.

Who, I ask, would be the first to receive him?

Now, as then, it would of course be the childlike in heart, the truest, the least selfish. They would not be the highest in the estimation of any church, for the childlike are not yet the many. It might not even be those that knew most about the former visit of the Master, or those who had pondered every word of the Greek Testament. It would not be the good churchman who would be first to cry, "It is the Lord!"

It would not be one with so little of the mind of Christ within him as to imagine the Lord caring about stupid outside matters. It would not be the man that holds by the mooring-ring of the letter, fast in the quay of what he calls theology, and from his rotting deck abuses the presumption of those that go down to the sea in ships. For such a one lets the wind of the Spirit blow where it will, but never allows it to blow him out among its wonders in the deep. It would not be he who, obeying a command, does not care to see reason in the command. It would not be he who, from very barrenness of soul, cannot receive the meaning and will of the Master, and therefore fails to fulfill the letter of his word, making it of no effect.

If any recognize him, it would certainly be those who are most like the Master—namely, those that do the will of their Father and his Father, who build their house on the rock by hearing and doing his sayings.

But are there any enough like him to immediately know him by the sound of his voice or by the look of his face? There are multitudes who would at once be taken by a false Christ fashioned according to their imagination, and would at once reject the Lord as a poor impostor. One thing is certain—they who first recognized him would be those that most loved righteousness and hated iniquity.

But I would not forget that there are many in whom foolish forms cover a live heart, warm toward everything human and divine. For the worst-fitting and ugliest robe may hide the loveliest form.

Every covering is not a clothing. The grass clothes the fields. The glory surpassing Solomon's clothes the grass. But the traditions of the worthiest elders will not clothe any soul—how much less the traditions of the unworthy! Its true clothing must grow out of the live soul itself.

Some naked souls need but the sight of truth to rush to it, as Dante says, like a wild beast to his den. Others, heavily clad in the garments the scribes have left behind them, and fearful of tearing the clothes of those traditions that are fit only to be trodden underfoot, approach the truth cautiously. They go round and round it like a shy horse that fears a hidden enemy.

But let each be true after the fashion possible to him, and he shall have the Master's praise.

If the Lord were to appear, the many who take the common presentation of a thing or person for the *actual* thing or person, could never recognize the new vision as another form of the old. The Master has been so misrepresented by such as have claimed to present him, and especially in the one eternal fact of facts—the relation between him and his Father—that it is impossible they should see any likeness between the reality and their image.

For my part, I would sooner believe in *no* God rather than in such a God as is generally offered for believing in. How far those may be to blame who, righteously disgusted, cast the idea from them without making inquiry whether *something* in it may possibly be true, though *most* must be false, it is not my work to inquire. Nor is it my business to ask whether any claim lies upon them to investigate the truth of the claims on the chance that some who call themselves God's prophets may have taken spiritual bribes . . .

> To mingle beauty with infirmities,
> And pure perfection with impure defeature

. . . and how much they may be to blame if they do not.

Some would grasp with gladness the hope that such chance might be proved a fact. Others would not care to discern in the story, written over by the ideas of men, covered but not obliterated, a credible tale of a perfect man revealing a perfect God.

They are not true enough to desire that to be fact which would immediately demand the modeling of their lives upon a perfect idea, and the founding of their every hope upon the same.

But we all, beholding the glory of the Lord, are changed into the same image, even the righteousness which is of God by faith.

Insights Into

THE KNOWING OF THE SON

MICHAEL PHILLIPS

THE PHANTOM OF
ABSOLUTE SCRIPTURAL LITERALITY

A great debate rages in certain Christian circles of our time over how one reads and interprets the words of the Bible—whether *literally* or not.

It is an unfortunate debate and a great waste of energy that produces more self-righteousness and judgment than insight into the true meaning of Scripture.

The fact is, no one takes the Bible "literally" all the time, nor "figuratively" all the time. We read literally when it suits our doctrinal bias, and figuratively when it does the same.

The most dyed-in-the-wool fundamentalist, who prides himself on literality, reads the Bible symbolically and interpretively when he needs to in order to preserve his fundamentalist doctrine. Likewise, the most contemporary liberal reads the Bible with strict literality when he needs to in order to preserve his liberal outlook. All we have to do is look at the communion passages of the New Testament, the book of Ecclesiastes, a few of Paul's cryptic epistles, and various prophetic sections of Daniel and Revelation to see clearly enough that we all mix and match literality and figurativeness in deciding how to read and interpret the Bible.

This was a principle George MacDonald understood well enough. His brief opening words in "The Knowing of the Son" (*Unspoken Sermons, Third Series*), in which he discusses his doubt that in the Gospels we are necessarily always reading the Lord's *exact* words, even raising minor doubts with regard to the disciples' memory of the Lord's precise words, strike a refreshing balance in the midst of today's obsession by some with the phantom of absolute literality. The practical and down-to-earth reality in MacDonald's observations feels good. We don't have to argue about such details. It is obvious that we are dealing with very old books that have come down to us with much potentiality for fluid memory on the part of the original authors, for scribal modification in later centuries, and even error. But the Spirit of God is at work in history. The mind of Christ is at work in his obedient disciples unto the discovery of truth. Let us therefore try to find what the texts *mean* in our lives. As always with MacDonald, it is a commonsense approach.

His words to the so-called "literalist" are as relevant today as they were to his readers then:

> God has not cared that we should anywhere have assurance of his precise words. The reason is not merely because of the tendency in his children toward word-worship, false logic, and corruption of the truth. It is also because he would not have them oppressed by words. Being human, words are but partially capable, and could not absolutely contain or express what the Lord meant. To be understood, even he must depend upon the spirit of his disciple. Seeing it could not give life, the letter should not be throned with power to kill. It should be but the handmaid to open the door of the truth to the mind that is *of* the truth.

As MacDonald goes on, nearly the first 30 to 40 percent of this essay might be called introductory. He continues to discuss how we are to discover truth from Scripture when we are not positively certain of the *precise* words. In so doing he discusses "individual inspiration" and interpretation, what to do when we do not understand, and the spirit required to be able to read Scripture aright amid these doubts of exactitude.

I have long been a student of the development of the New Testament and its documents, as well as the historical process of canonization. My reading in this area helps place the biblical books in their historical and spiritual context. It demythologizes many individuals on whose heads we are a little overzealous to place halos. The process by which the Bible has come to us is not as smooth as one might think.

Though I confess I have read next to nothing of them, I have long known of the Dead Sea Scrolls, discovered at Qumran in 1947. But my familiarity with the Nag Hammadi Texts, found south of Cairo two years earlier, had been far sketchier. I had heard of but one, the so-called "Gospel According to Thomas," a collection of sayings reported to be those of the Lord and purportedly of ancient date from the hand of the Lord's disciple. Though liberal scholars hail the discovery of these mostly Gnostic Christian texts as authentic and as shedding valuable new light on Jesus and his teachings, as recently I read through this "gospel" it was obvious to me that its "light" is cast from a very different direction than the light from John's gospel.

Concerning the discovery of truth and a right knowing of Jesus, MacDonald says, "I have yet seen no words credibly reported as the words of Jesus concerning which I dared to say, 'His mind is not therein.'" Reading "The Gospel According to Thomas," I *do* dare say about many of its sayings that Christ's mind is not therein. Therefore I must question, to borrow MacDonald's word, the "credibility" of the report.

My experience with this alternate "sayings-gospel" makes so alive and relevant his discussion about how we see and how we discern what "words embody the mind of Christ" as he said John's words did to him. We must look beyond the words . . . to the spirit behind them.

And when one delves into the "spirit" of many Gnostic

texts, it becomes clear indeed what a very different spirit is in them than the Spirit of Christ.

KNOWING JESUS BY BEING TRUE

Once he begins his actual discussion about "the knowing of the Son," we see toward what MacDonald's introductory remarks have been pointed. We cannot know of a certainty the Lord's precise words. We must learn to "know truth" in them from discerning their spirit rather than analyzing their letter.

Furthermore, we must read them from deeper places within ourselves, by *being* true. In the same way, we also come to "know" Christ not by *seeing* him but by probing deeper.

We come to know by the spirit, not the letter . . . through the heart, not the eyes. A right spirit is required both for *understanding* and *knowing*—the Spirit of Christ himself. Without his spirit, we can neither understand the words he spoke nor know him as he is to be known.

With that spirit, we penetrate what MacDonald calls the unseen.

The heavens and the earth are around us that it may be possible for us to speak of the unseen by the seen. For the outermost husk of creation has correspondence with the deepest things of the Creator. He is not a God that hides himself, but a God who *made* that he might *reveal. . . .*

There are things with which an enemy hath meddled. But there are more things with which no enemy can meddle. . . . They may not have revealed him fully to us, but at least when he *is* revealed, they will show themselves so much of his nature that we will at once recognize and use them as spiritual tokens in the commerce of the Spirit. . . .

If Jesus said these precise words, he meant more, not less, than lies on their surface.

MacDonald now turns to begin his exposition of the passage from John's gospel under consideration: Jesus' condemnation of the Jews for not knowing either him or his Father.

The word *see* is used in one sense in the one statement, and in another sense in the other. In the one it means *see with the eyes*. In the other, *with the soul*. The one statement is made about all men, the other is made to certain of the Jews of Jerusalem concerning themselves. . . . No man has seen him [God] with his *bodily* eyes; these Jews ought to have seen him with their *spiritual* eyes.

No man has ever seen God in any outward, visible, close-fitting form of his own. . . . But multitudes of men have with their *mind's*—or rather their *heart's*—eye, seen more or less of God. And perhaps every man *might have* and *ought to have* seen something of him.

They have not seen or heard. But they ought to have.

The reproach in the words of the Lord is the reproach of men who *ought* to have had an experience they had not had. . . . *You do not know what he is like.*

Plainly he implies, *You ought to know his voice. You ought to know what he is like.*

Why were they unseeing and unknowing? Because God's will was not at home in their hearts.

The argument of the Lord was indeed of small weight with . . . those to whom it most applied. For the more it applied, the more incapable they were of seeing that it did apply. . . .

His argument was this:

"If you had ever heard the Father's voice . . . if you had cared for his will so that his word was at home in your hearts, then you would have known me when you saw me. . . . Thus, you would have listened to me.

"The least acquaintance with God, such as any true heart must have, would have made you recognize that I came from God. . . . You would have seen my Father in me. You would have known me by the little you knew of him. The family-feeling would have been awake in you, the holy instinct of the same spirit, making you know your elder brother. . . .

"If you had loved my Father, you would have known his Son."

WOULD WE RECOGNIZE HIM TODAY?

MacDonald then sends the argument from the Jews of old straight into our own lives, asking what the Lord would look like if he now appeared among us.

If the Lord were to appear this day in England as he once did in Palestine, he would not come in the halo of the painters, or with that wintry shine of effeminate beauty and sweet weakness in which it is their helpless custom to represent him. . . . He would come in such form and condition as might bear to the present England, Scotland, and Ireland, a relation like that which the form and condition he then came in bore to the motley Judea, Samaria, and Galilee.

And the jolting question:

If he came thus, in a form altogether unlooked for, who would they be who would recognize and receive him? . . .

Now, as then, it would of course be the childlike in heart, the truest, the least selfish. They would not be the highest in the estimation of any church. . . . It might not even be those that knew most about the former visit of the Master, or those who had pondered every word of the Greek Testament. It would not be the good churchman who would be first to cry, "It is the Lord!" . . .

If any recognize him, it would certainly be those who are most like the Master—namely, those that do the will of their Father and his Father.

Finally, MacDonald closes on a personal note concerning his own knowing of the Son.

For my part, I would sooner believe in *no* God rather than in such a God as is generally offered for believing in. How far those may be to blame who, righteously disgusted, cast the idea from them without making inquiry whether *something* in it may possibly be true, though *most* must be false, it is not my work to inquire. Nor is it my business to ask whether any claim lies upon them to investigate the truth of the claims.

The truth in Jesus comes from knowing Jesus truly, as MacDonald says in summary, from grasping the hope of that truth with gladness out of the "credible tale of a perfect man revealing a perfect God."

RIGHTEOUSNESS

GEORGE MACDONALD

*That I may win Christ, and be found in him, not having
mine own righteousness, which is of the law, but that which
is through the faith of Christ, the righteousness
which is of God by faith.*

—PHILIPPIANS 3:8–9

What does the apostle Paul mean by *the righteousness
which is of God by faith* in Philippians 3:9? He means the
same righteousness Christ had by his faith in God, the same
righteousness God himself has.

In his second epistle to the Corinthians, Paul says, "He
hath made him to be sin for us who knew no sin, that we
might be made the righteousness of God in him" (5:21). This
is read by some as "He gave him to be treated like a sinner,

killed and cast out of his own vineyard by his husbandmen, that we might in him be made righteous like God."

As the antithesis in the verse stands it is rhetorically correct. But if the former half means *"He made him to be treated as if he were a sinner,"* then the latter half should, in logical precision, mean *"That we might be treated as if we were righteous."*

THE LEGAL FICTION OF
THE DOCTRINE OF IMPUTATION

"That is just what Paul does mean," insist not a few. "He means that Jesus was treated by God as if he were a sinner, our sins being imputed to him, in order that we might be treated as if we were righteous, his righteousness being imputed to us."

In other words, by a sort of legal fiction, Jesus was treated as what *he was not*, in order that we might be treated as what *we are not*. This is the best device, according to the prevailing theology, that the God of truth—the God of mercy, whose glory is that he is just to men by forgiving their sins—could devise to save his creatures!

I had thought that this most contemptible of false doctrines would have by now ceased to be presented, though I knew it would be long before it ceased to exercise its baneful influence. But to my astonishment I came upon it recently in quite a modern commentary which I happened to look into in a friend's house. I say *to my astonishment* because the commentary was the work of one of the most liberal and lovely of Christians, a dignitary high in the church of England, a man whom I knew and love and hope before long to meet where there are no churches. In the comment that came under my eye, he refers to the doctrine of imputed righteousness as the possible explanation of a certain passage. He refers to it as if it is a doctrine whose truth was not even so much as in question.

It seems to me, seeing how much duplicity exists in the body of Christ, that every honest member of it should protest against any word tending to imply the existence of falsehood in the indwelling spirit of that body.

Therefore, I now offer my protest against this so-called *doctrine*. I count it the rightful prey of the foolishest wind in the limbo of vanities, whither I would gladly do my best to send it. It is a mean, nauseous invention, false, and productive of falsehood.

If you say it is only a "picture" of truth, I will answer that it is not only a false one but an embodiment of untruth. If you say that it expresses a reality, I say it teaches the worst of lies. If you say that there is a shadow of truth in it, I answer it may be so, but there is no truth touched in it that could not be taught infinitely better without it.

It is the meager, misshapen offspring of the legalism of a poverty-stricken mechanical fancy, unlighted by a gleam of divine imagination. No one who knows his New Testament will dare to say that the figure is once used in it.

I have dealt already with the source from which the doctrine comes. They say first that God must punish the sinner, for justice requires it. Then they say that he does *not* punish the sinner but punishes a perfectly righteous man instead—attributing that man's righteousness to the sinner—and by such a means God's justice is not compromised.

Was there ever such a confusion, such an inversion of right and wrong!

Justice *could not* treat a righteous man as unrighteous. Neither, if justice required the punishment of sin, *could* justice let the sinner go unpunished. Justice is plainly compromised—and on both sides of the argument.

To lay the pain upon the righteous in the name of justice is simply monstrous. No wonder unbelief is rampant. Believe in Molech if you will, but call him Molech, not Justice.

Be sure that the thing that God gives—the righteousness that is of God—is a real thing, and not a contemptible legalism. Pray God I have no righteousness imputed to me. Let me be regarded as the sinner I am, for nothing will serve my need but to be made a *truly* righteous man, one that will sin no more.

IMPUTATION IN THE BIBLE

We have the word *imputed* just once in the New Testament. Whether the evil doctrine may have sprung from any possible misunderstanding of the passage where it occurs, I hardly care to inquire. The word as Paul uses it, and the whole of the thought from which his use of it springs, appeals to my sense of right and justice as much as the common use of it arouses my abhorrence.

The apostle says that a certain thing was imputed to Abraham for righteousness. Or, as the revised version has it, "reckoned unto him."[1]

What was it that was thus imputed to Abraham? The righteousness of another? God forbid! It was his *own* faith. The faith *of Abraham* is reckoned to him for righteousness.

To impute the righteousness of one to another is simply to act a falsehood. To call the faith of a man his righteousness is simply to speak the truth. Was it not righteous of Abraham to obey God?

The Jews considered righteousness to be keeping all the particulars of the law of Moses. But Paul says faith in God was counted as righteousness before Moses was even born.

You may answer, "Abraham was unjust in many things, and by no means a righteous man."

True. He was not a righteous man in any complete sense. His righteousness would never have satisfied Paul. Neither, you may be sure, did it satisfy Abraham. But his *faith* was nevertheless righteousness, and if it had not been counted to him as righteousness, there would have been falsehood somewhere. For such faith as Abraham's *is righteousness*.

Abraham's faith was no mere intellectual recognition of the existence of a God, which is consistent with the deepest atheism. It was that *faith which is one with action*: "He went out, not knowing whither he went."

The very act of believing in God in such a way that, when the time for action comes, the man will obey God, is the highest act, the deepest, loftiest righteousness of which man

---

[1]Revised Version, 1885.

is capable. Such *obedience* is at the root of all other righteousness. And the spirit of such obedience will work till the man is perfect.

FAITH: THE BEGINNING OF RIGHTEOUSNESS

If you define righteousness in the common sense, that is, in the divine fashion—for religion is nothing if it be not the deepest common sense—as giving to everyone his due, then certainly the first due is to him who makes us capable of owing, that is, makes us responsible creatures.

You may say this is not one's first feeling of duty. True—but the first in reality is seldom the first perceived. The first duty is too high and too deep to be the first one that comes into consciousness. If anyone were born perfect, which I count an eternal impossibility, then the highest duty would come first into the consciousness. As we are born imperfect, it is the doing of, or at least the honest trying to do many another duty that will at length lead a man to see that his duty to God is the first and deepest and highest of all.

Our duty to God includes and requires the performance of all other duties whatever. A man might live a thousand years in neglect of duty and never come to see that any obligation was upon him to put faith in God and do what he told him—never have a glimpse of the fact that he owed God something. I will allow that if God were what such a one thinks him, the man would indeed owe him little. But he thinks him such because he has not done what he knows he ought to do. He has not come to the light. He has deadened, dulled, and hardened his nature. He has not been a man without guile. He has not been true and fair.

But while faith in God is the first duty—and may therefore well be called righteousness in one in whom it is operative though imperfect—there is more reason than this why it should be counted to a man for righteousness. Faith is the one spiritual act which brings man into contact with the original creative power who made him—the One who is able to help him in every endeavour toward righteousness and ensure his progress to perfection.

The man who exercises faith may therefore also well be called a righteous man, however far from *complete* in righteousness. We may call a woman beautiful who is not perfect in beauty. In the Bible men are constantly recognized as righteous men who are far from *perfectly* righteous.

The Bible never deals with impossibilities. God never demands of any man or woman at any given moment a righteousness of which at that moment he or she is incapable. Neither does the Bible lay upon man any other law than that of perfect righteousness.

It demands of him righteousness. When he yields that righteousness *of which he is capable*, content for the moment, it goes on to demand *more*.

The common sense of the Bible is lovely.

GROWING GRADUALLY INTO LIFE-RIGHTEOUSNESS

To the man who has no faith in God, faith in God cannot look like righteousness. Neither can he know that it is creative of all other righteousness toward equal and inferior lives. He cannot know that it is not merely the beginning of righteousness but the germ of life, the active potency out of which life-righteousness grows. It is not like some single separate act of righteousness, it is the action of the whole man, turning himself to good and away from evil. Life-righteousness is turning one's back on all that is opposed to righteousness and starting on a road on which he cannot stop, in which he must go on growing more and more righteous, discovering more and more what righteousness is, and more and more what is unrighteous in himself.

In the one act of believing in God—that is, of giving himself to do what he tells him—a man abjures evil, both what he knows and what he does not yet know in himself. A man may indeed have turned to obey God and yet be capable of many an injustice to his neighbour which he has not yet discovered to be an injustice. But as he continues to obey, he will continue to discover truth. Not only will he grow more and more determined to be just, but he will grow more and more sensitive to the idea of injustice—not in others, but in himself.

A man who continues capable of a known injustice to his neighbour cannot be believed to have turned to God. In any event, a man cannot be near God, so as to be learning what is just toward God, and not be near his neighbour, so as to be learning what is unfair to him. For his own will, which is the deepest in him, lays hold of righteousness and *chooses* to be righteous.

If a man is to be blamed for not choosing righteousness,

for not turning to the light, for not coming out of the darkness, then the man who does choose and turn and come out is to be justified in his deed and declared to be righteous. He is not yet *thoroughly* righteous, but he is *growing in* and *toward* righteousness.

He needs creative God, and time for will and effort. Not yet *quite* righteous, he cannot yet act quite righteously, for only the man in whom the image of God is perfected can live perfectly. Born into the world without righteousness, he cannot see, he cannot know, he is not in touch with perfect righteousness. It would be the deepest injustice to demand of him, with a penalty, at any given moment, more than he knows how to yield. But it is the highest love constantly to demand of him perfect righteousness as what he must attain to. With what life and possibility is in him, he must keep turning to righteousness and abjuring iniquity, ever aiming at the perfection of God.

Such an obedient faith is most justly and fairly, being all that God himself can require of the man, called by God "righteousness" in the man. This would not be enough for the righteousness of God, or Jesus, or any perfected saint, because they are capable of perfect righteousness, and, knowing what is perfect righteousness, choose to be perfectly righteous. But in virtue of the life and growth in it, such is enough at a given moment for the disciple of the Perfect.

The righteousness of Abraham could not be compared with the righteousness of Paul. He did not fight with himself for righteousness as did Paul—not because he was better than Paul and therefore did not need to fight, but because his idea of what was required of him was not within sight of that of Paul. Yet Abraham was righteous in the same way as Paul was righteous—he had *begun* to be righteous, and God called his righteousness *righteousness*, for faith is righteousness. His faith was an act of recognizing God as his law, and that is not a *partial* act but an all-embracing and all-determining action.

A single righteous deed toward one's fellow could hardly be imputed to a man as righteousness. A man who is not trying to be righteous may yet do many a righteous act. Such acts will not be forgotten to him, yet neither will they be imputed to him as righteousness.

Abraham's action of obedient faith was righteousness nonetheless that his righteousness was far behind Paul's. Abraham started at the beginning of the long, slow, disappointing preparation of the Jewish people. Paul started at its close, with the story of Jesus behind him. Both *believed*, obeying God, and therefore both were *righteous*. They were righteous because they gave themselves up to God to make them righteous. Not to call such men righteous, not to impute their faith to them for righteousness, would be unjust. But God is utterly just, and nowise resembles a legal-minded Roman emperor or a bad pope formulating the doctrine of vicarious sacrifice.

GOD'S RIGHTEOUSNESS OF FAITH

What, then, is the righteousness which is of God by faith? It is simply the thing that God wants every man to be, wrought out in him by constant obedient contact with God himself. It is not an attribute either of God or man, but *a fact of character* in God and in man.

It is God's righteousness wrought out in us, so that as he is righteous we too are righteous. It does not consist in obeying this or that law. It does not even consist in the keeping of every law. Even no hairsbreadth running counter to one of God's laws would make us righteous.

To be righteous is to be such a heart, soul, mind, and will as, without regard to law, would recoil with horror from the lightest possible breach of any law.

It is to be so in love with what is fair and right as to make it impossible for a man to do anything that is less than absolutely righteous.

It is not the love of righteousness in the abstract that makes anyone righteous, but such a love of fair play toward everyone with whom we come into contact that anything less than the fulfilling, with a clear joy, of our divine relation to him or her is impossible.

For the righteousness of God goes far beyond mere *deeds*, and requires of us love and helping mercy as our highest obligation and justice to our fellowmen—those of them too who have done nothing for us, those even who have done us wrong.

Our relations with others, God first and then our neighbour in order and degree, must one day *become*, as in true nature they *are*, the gladness of our being. Nothing will then ever appear good for us that is not in harmony with those blessed relations. Every thought will not merely be *just*, but will be just because it is something more, because it is *live* and *true*.

What heart in the kingdom of heaven would ever dream of constructing a metaphysical system of what we owed to God and why we owed it? The light of our life—our sole, eternal, and infinite joy—is simply God—God—God—nothing but God, and all his creatures in him. He is all and in all, and the children of the kingdom know it. He includes all things. It is untrue to him to be untrue to anything he has made. God is truth, he is life. To be in God is to know him and need no law. Existence will be eternal Godness.

Does it seem that you would not like such a way of life? There is, there can be, no other. But before you can determine what it would be like, you must know at least a little of God as he *is*, not as you imagine him.

I say *as you imagine him* because it cannot be that any creature should know him as he is and not desire him. In proportion as we know him we must desire him, until at length we live in and for him with all our conscious heart. That is why the Jews did not like the Lord—he cared so simply for his Father's will and not for anything they called his will.

The righteousness which is *of God by faith* in the source, the prime of that righteousness, is then just the same kind as *God's* righteousness, differing only as the created differs from the creating. The righteousness of him who does the will of his Father in heaven is the righteousness of Jesus Christ—it is God's own righteousness. The righteousness which is of God by faith in God is *God's* righteousness.

The man who has this righteousness thinks about things as

God thinks about them, loves the things that *God* loves, cares for nothing that *God* does not care about. Even while this righteousness is being born in him, the man will say to himself, "Why should I be troubled about this thing or that? Does God care about it? No. Then why should I care? I must not care. I will not care!"

If he does not know whether God cares about it or not, he will say, "If God cares that I should have what I desire, he will give it me. If he does not want me to have it, neither will I care. In the meantime I will do my work."

The man with God's righteousness does not love a thing merely because it is right, but loves the very rightness in it. He not only loves a thought, but he loves the man in his thinking that thought—he loves the thought alive in the man. He does not take his joy from himself. He feels joy in himself—from God first, and from somebody, anybody, everybody next. He would rather, in the fullness of his contentment, cease to exist himself than that another should. He could do without knowing himself, but he could not know himself and spare one of the brothers or sisters God had given him.

The man who really knows God is, and always will be, content with what God, who is the very self of his self, shall choose for him. He is entirely God's, and not at all his own. His consciousness of himself is the reflex from those about him, not the result of the turning in of his own regard upon himself. His joy comes not from contemplating what God has made him, but in *being* what God has made him, and contemplating what *God himself is* and what he has made his fellows.

He wants nothing, and feels that he has all things, for he is in the bosom of his Father, and the thoughts of his Father come to him. He knows that if he needs anything, it is his before he asks it. For his Father has willed him, in the might and truth of his fatherhood, to be one with himself.

THE CHILD'S REJECTION OF A FALSE MESSENGER

This then, or something like this—for words are poor to tell the best things—is the righteousness which is of God by faith. It is so far from being a thing built of the rubbish heap of legal fiction called *vicarious sacrifice*, or its shadow called *imputed righteousness*, that only the child with a child-heart, so far ahead of and so different from those who think themselves wise and prudent, can understand it.

Those who think themselves wise and prudent interpret God by themselves, and do not understand him. The child interprets God by himself, and does understand him. The wise and prudent must make a system and arrange things to their minds before they can say *I believe*. The child sees, believes, obeys—and knows he must be perfect as his Father in heaven is perfect.

If an angel, seeming to come from heaven, told such a child that God had let him off, that he did not require so much of him as righteousness but would be content with less, he would not believe it. If he went on to tell the child that, though God could not indeed allow him to be wicked, he loved him so dearly that he would pass by a great deal, modifying his demands because it was so hard for him to be completely good, the child of God would at once recognize, woven with the angel's starry brilliancy, the flicker of the flames of hell, and would say to the shining one, "Get thee behind me, Satan."

Nor would there be the slightest wonder or merit in his doing so, for at the words of the deceiver, if but for briefest moment imagined true, the shadow of a rising hell would gloom over the face of creation. Hope would vanish. The eternal would be as the carcass of a dead man. The glory would die out of the face of God, until the groan of a thunderous *No!* burst from the caverns of the universe, and the truth, flashing on his child's soul from the heart of the Eternal, Immortal, Invisible, withered up the lie of the messenger of darkness.

How God Brings Righteousness About in Us

"But how," you ask, "can God bring this about in me?"

Let him do it, and perhaps you will know. If you never know, yet there it will be. Help him to do it, or he cannot do it.

He originates the possibility of your being his son, his daughter. He makes you *able* to will it, but you must *will* it.

If he is not doing it in you—that is, if you have as yet prevented him from beginning, why should I tell you, even if I knew the process, how he would do what you will not let him do? Why should you know? What claim have you to know? But indeed how should you be able to know? For it must deal with deeper and higher things than you *can* know anything of until the work is at least begun. Perhaps if you approved of the plans of the glad Creator, you would allow him to make of you something divine! To teach your intellect what has to be learned by your whole being, what cannot be understood without the whole being, what it would do you no good to understand except you understood it in your whole being—if this be the province of any man, it is not mine. Let the dead bury their dead, and the dead teach their dead. For me, I will try to wake them.

To those who are awake, I cry, "For the sake of your Father and the firstborn among many brethren to whom we belong, for the sake of those he has given us to love the most dearly, let patience have her perfect work. Statue under the chisel of the Sculptor, stand steady to the blows of his mallet. Clay on the wheel, let the fingers of the Divine Potter model you at their will. Obey the Father's lightest word. Hear the Brother who knows you, and died for you. Beat down your sin, and trample it to death."

Brother, sister, when you sit at home in your house, which is the temple of the Lord, open all your windows to breathe the air of his approach. Set the watcher on your turret that he may listen out into the dark for the sound of his coming, and your hand be on the latch to open the door at his first knock. Should you open the door and not see him, do not say he did not knock, but understand that he is there, and wants you to go out to him. It may be he has something for you to do for him. Go and do it, and perhaps you will return with a new prayer, to find a new window in your soul.

Never wait for a fitter time or place to talk to him. To wait till you go to church, or to your closet, is to make *him* wait. He will listen as you walk in the lane or the crowded street, on the commons or in the place of shining concourse.

Remember, if indeed you are able to know it, that the service he requires is not done in any church. He will say to no man, "You never went to church, depart from me—I do not know you." But he will say, "Inasmuch as you never helped one of my Father's children, you have done nothing for me."

Church is *not* the place for divine service. It is a place of prayer, a place of praise, a place to feed upon good things, a place to learn of God, as what place is not? It is a place to look into the eyes of your neighbour, and love God along with him. But the world in which you move, the place of your living and loving and labour, not the church you go to on your holy day, is the place of divine service. Serve your neighbour, and you serve God.

Do not heed much if men mock you and speak lies of you, or in goodwill defend you unworthily. Heed not much if even the seeming righteous turn their backs upon you. Only take heed that you turn not from them.

Insights Into

RIGHTEOUSNESS

MICHAEL PHILLIPS

Once again the pen of George MacDonald ploughs deep into the hard ground of Protestant orthodoxy, upturning one of the most sacred doctrines in all reformed theology—the doctrine of imputed righteousness.

If MacDonald has his occasional "signature turns" that repeat themselves in his writings, he also has several doctrinal bees in his bonnet that he will speak against—in the strongest language—at every opportunity.

This is one of them.

It is the doctrine that says we will never really *be* righteous, but that righteousness will be imputed or ascribed to us *as if* we were . . . yet all the while our sinfulness remains.

The very idea was odious to him, striking at the very heart of God's eternal plan in the creation. For MacDonald, imputed righteousness removes the essential power from the atonement itself.

GEORGE MACDONALD'S OUTRAGE

Unbelief, if honestly held, never upset MacDonald. Indeed, one always senses an affection, even admiration, for the thinking, honest skeptic. With such a one he will discuss, will occasionally debate, will often challenge, but will never condemn.

George MacDonald did, however, condemn what he calls *unbelief* in the church, condemned it all the more stringently in that it went by the name of "belief." The unbelief of believers who held to the vilest of falsehoods in place of true belief, believing ideas about God that were nothing short of blasphemies against his true nature—such unbelief truly raised MacDonald's ire. He termed such doctrines "legal fiction," foremost among which ("the most contemptible of false doctrines") was that of imputed righteousness.

> Seeing how much duplicity exists in the body of Christ . . . every honest member of it should protest against any word tending to imply the existence of falsehood in the indwelling spirit of that body.
>
> Therefore, I now offer my protest against this so-called *doctrine*. . . . It is a mean, nauseous invention, false, and productive of falsehood.

If you say it is only a "picture" of truth, I will answer that it is not only a false one but an embodiment of untruth. If you say that it expresses a reality, I say it teaches the worst of lies. . . .

It is the meager, misshapen offspring of the legalism of a poverty-stricken mechanical fancy, unlighted by a gleam of divine imagination. No one who knows his New Testament will dare to say that the figure is once used in it.

There is something wonderfully human in his casual reference to being at a friend's house and happening to look into a commentary he saw there. One gets a few personal glimpses into MacDonald's daily life. All the more, therefore, do I love this image: the conversation flags . . . his friend is distracted or called away momentarily . . . MacDonald's eyes scan the room . . . unconsciously he wanders toward the bookcase . . . he begins to note the spines of its contents . . . ah, a new commentary by so-and-so. . . .

His mind was continually on the lookout for new ideas and fresh perspectives. By the time his friend returns with the tea tray, there is MacDonald sunk in a chair, book open in his lap, deep in thought, poring over the author's comments on some favorite passage.

Am I reading too much between the lines? Perhaps. And yet is it not exactly what many bibliophiles would do with a spare minute on their hands in a room filled with books?

And in the briefly borrowed commentary MacDonald finds the phrase that brings his blood to a boil on behalf of truth.

An even more important insight exists for us in his sharing

of this incident. That is the ease with which "accepted" doctrines find their way into the mainstream of Christian consciousness, passed down without anyone's pausing to subject them to the scrutiny of Scripture or the character of God.

MacDonald's comment here could not more aptly describe the unthinking acceptance of much Christian doctrine in our own time, even as it did in his: "He refers to it as if it is a doctrine whose truth was not even so much as in question."

Then follows the challenge that honest Christians should "protest against any word tending to imply the existence of falsehood."

Therefore MacDonald *will* protest.

In brief, the doctrine he comes against here, so fundamental to the Calvinist view of the atonement, is that Jesus will be treated *as if* he were a sinner so that we will be let off, treated *as if* we are righteous.

The illogic of it, the very affront of it to the character of a God who would even consider such an arrangement, infuriated MacDonald almost as much as that Christians could swallow it without batting an eye.

In other words, by a sort of legal fiction, Jesus was treated as what *he was not*, in order that we might be treated as what *we are not*. This is the best device, according to the prevailing theology, that the God of truth—the God of mercy, whose glory is that he is just to men by forgiving their sins—could devise to save his creatures!

MacDonald then goes on to outline the "legal fiction" by

which the doctrine has come to be based on a contorted image of God's justice. It is not the only place in his writings he does so, but this succinct summary of strong feeling on the matter is important enough to bear repeating.

They say first that God must punish the sinner, for justice requires it. Then they say that he does *not* punish the sinner, but punishes a perfectly righteous man instead—attributing that man's righteousness to the sinner—and by such a means God's justice is not compromised.

Was there ever such a confusion, such an inversion of right and wrong!

Justice *could not* treat a righteous man as an unrighteous. Neither, if justice required the punishment of sin, *could* justice let the sinner go unpunished. Justice is plainly compromised—and on both sides of the argument.

To lay the pain upon the righteous in the name of justice is simply monstrous. No wonder unbelief is rampant. Believe in Molech if you will, but call him Molech, not Justice.

What an illuminating cry from MacDonald's pained heart: *No wonder unbelief is rampant.*

Surely thinking, serious Christian men and women echo it in our own day. If Christians explain what they call "God's love" by such means as to make God out to be as cruel as Molech (a Canaanite deity to whom children were sacrificed), no less today than in the black Scottish Calvinism of that time, no wonder unbelief is rampant now as well. To believe the "gospel" as commonly presented requires abandoning logic, common sense, and a sense of true "justice" altogether.

But there is an even more illuminating cry from George MacDonald's heart. Here we penetrate perhaps to the very depths of much that explains why MacDonald grasped truth as deeply as he did, and what distinguished him from most theologians of his time or any time. The deepest hunger of his being was not merely to be "saved" to slip through the gates of heaven without regard for how it was done or how many were left out or even without serious regard for the state of his own soul . . . just so long as he had performed the formula correctly to make sure that his own sin was passed over and "atoned" for.

Such a "salvation" could never satisfy MacDonald. We have hints, in *Robert Falconer* in particular, that it failed to satisfy him from an early age. MacDonald hungered to be righteous himself, not to have his sins covered over by a "legal fiction" and pretended to be other than they were. His desire was really to become righteous (which hunger he here also claims on behalf of Abraham and Paul).

Most Christians, it seems, want only to get "in," to be *saved* without having to become righteous. If such is one's goal, the contortion of Calvinism's atonement will do fine.

But it would not do for George MacDonald. He would not have the sin within him merely glossed over. He would have it utterly conquered.

> Be sure that the thing that God gives—the righteous-
> ness that is of God—is a real thing, and not a contempt-
> ible legalism. Pray God I have no righteousness imputed

to me. Let me be regarded as the sinner I am, for nothing will serve my need but to be made a *truly* righteous man, one that will sin no more.

WHAT IS RIGHTEOUSNESS?

MacDonald then goes on to investigate the word *imputed* as used in the New Testament. He clarifies its meaning as the very opposite from that implied by the common imputation doctrine of the atonement.

> What was it that was thus imputed to Abraham? The righteousness of another? God forbid! It was his *own* faith. The faith *of Abraham* is reckoned to him for righteousness.
> To impute the righteousness of one to another is simply to act a falsehood.

Since it is *faith* that is counted to Abraham as "righteousness," MacDonald inquires into the true nature of both, saying that faith is the beginning of righteousness.

> The very act of believing in God in such a way that, when the time for action comes, the man will obey God, is the highest act, the deepest, loftiest righteousness of which man is capable. Such *obedience* is at the root of all other righteousness. . . .
> But while faith in God is the first duty . . . there is more reason than this why it should be counted to a man for righteousness. Faith is the one spiritual act which

brings man into contact with the original creative power who made him.

He adds that righteousness does not imply perfection but faith to *begin* being righteous, that is, for a man to obey the first call of righteousness of which he is capable, that he might grow capable of more.

> The man who exercises faith may therefore also well be called a righteous man, however far from *complete* in righteousness. . . . In the Bible men are constantly recognized as righteous men who are far from *perfectly* righteous.
>
> The Bible never deals with impossibilities. God never demands of any man or woman at any given moment a righteousness of which at that moment he or she is incapable. Neither does the Bible lay upon man any other law than that of perfect righteousness.
>
> It demands of him righteousness. When he yields that righteousness *of which he is capable*, content for the moment, it goes on to demand *more*.
>
> The common sense of the Bible is lovely.

In a few brief paragraphs MacDonald gives us as close to a "definition" as he ever gives to high spiritual things. It is not something he is wont to do—one has to ferret out such little gems—but in these passages, perhaps we discover several of such principles.

First, *duty*, or man's highest duty:

> Our duty to God includes and requires the perform-

ance of all other duties whatever . . . to put faith in God and do what he told him.

Second, *righteousness*. What exactly is "righteousness"?

> The beginning of righteousness . . . the germ of life, the active potency out of which life-righteousness grows . . . is the action of the whole man, turning himself to good and away from evil. Life-righteousness is turning one's back on all that is opposed to righteousness . . . discovering more and more what righteousness is, and more and more what is unrighteous in himself.

Third, *belief*. What exactly is "belief" in God, according to MacDonald?

> The one act of believing in God—that is, of giving himself to do what he tells him. . . . As he continues to obey, he will continue to discover truth.

Finally, he defines "the righteousness which is of God by faith."

> It is to be so in love with what is fair and right as to make it impossible for a man to do anything that is less than absolutely righteous . . . such a love of fair play toward everyone with whom we come into contact, that anything less than the fulfilling, with a clear joy, of our divine relation to him or her, is impossible.
> For the righteousness of God goes far beyond mere *deeds*, and requires of us love and helping mercy as our highest obligation and justice to our fellowmen. . . .

The man who has this righteousness thinks about things as *God* thinks about them, loves the things that *God* loves, cares for nothing that *God* does not care about. . . .

He wants nothing, and feels that he has all things, for he is in the bosom of his Father, and the thoughts of his Father come to him.

A frequent theme for MacDonald is the distinction he makes between any spiritual ideal and the growth toward that ideal. In the growth toward it, if it is earnest, sincere, honest, and humble growth, he says that God receives it as the perfected potential of the perfected ideal. And then, having received it, God always urges his growing son or daughter yet higher toward the perfect.

So here he insists that God continually calls to higher and higher righteousness. We are reminded of his *Easy he is to please, but hard to satisfy.*

The man who does choose and turn . . . is not yet *thoroughly* righteous, but he is *growing in* and *toward* righteousness. . . . It is the highest love constantly to demand of him perfect righteousness. . . . He must keep turning to righteousness . . . ever aiming at the perfection of God.

Such an obedient faith . . . would not be enough for the righteousness of God, or Jesus, or any perfected saint. . . . But in virtue of the life and growth in it, such is enough at a given moment. . . .

The righteousness of Abraham could not be compared with the righteousness of Paul. . . . Yet Abraham was righteous in the same way as Paul was righteous—he had *begun* to be righteous.

THE TRUE AND THE FALSE

Again MacDonald contrasts these wonderful tidings of what God purposes to accomplish within us with the commonly taught orthodoxy:

> This then, or something like this—for words are poor to tell the best things—is the righteousness which is of God by faith. It is so far from being a thing built of the rubbish heap of legal fiction called *vicarious sacrifice*, or its shadow called *imputed righteousness*, that only the child with a child-heart, so far ahead of and so different from those who think themselves wise and prudent, can understand it.

It is only the spiritually childlike—those who want their whole heart to be righteous, not to have their unrighteousness covered up by means of a doctrine that says they can get away with being less than perfect—who can truly see the truth of God's righteousness by faith.

> Those who think themselves wise and prudent interpret God . . . and do not understand him. The child . . . does understand him. The wise and prudent must make a system and arrange things to their minds before they can say, *I believe*. The child sees, believes, obeys—and knows he must be perfect as his Father in heaven is perfect.

And then the all-important *how*. How can such faith, and its righteousness, possibly be effected in us, still less *perfected* in us?

> But how . . . can God bring this about . . . ?
>
> Let him do it, and perhaps you will know. . . . Help him to do it, or he cannot do it.
>
> He originates the possibility of your being his son, his daughter. He makes you *able* to will it, but you must *will* it. . . .
>
> To those who are awake, I cry . . . "Statue under the chisel of the Sculptor, stand steady to the blows of his mallet. Clay on the wheel, let the fingers of the Divine Potter model you at their will. Obey the Father's lightest word. Hear the Brother who knows you, and died for you. Beat down your sin, and trample it to death."

MacDonald closes with what may be for some an unsettling admonishment. (Church worshipers existed in his day as they do in our own—not those who worship God in church, I mean, but those who worship church instead of serving God.)

> Brother, sister, when you sit at home in your house, which is the temple of the Lord, open all your windows to breathe the air of his approach. . . . It may be he has something for you to do for him. Go and do it, and perhaps you will return with a new prayer, to find a new window in your soul.
>
> . . . The service he requires is not done in any church. He will say to no man, "You never went to church, depart

from me—I do not know you." But he will say, "Inasmuch as you never helped one of my father's children, you have done nothing for me."

May we be bold not only to think courageously about Jesus and his truth, as George MacDonald did, but also to serve God as he challenges us in the world in which we move, the place of our living and loving and labor.

THE AUTHORS

George MacDonald
(1824–1905), Scottish
Victorian novelist, began
his adult life as a clergy-
man and always consid-
ered himself a poet first
of all. His unorthodox
views resulted in a very
short career in the pul-
pit in the early 1850s,
after which he turned to
writing in earnest. He
initially attracted notice
for poetry and his adult

fantasy *Phantastes* (1855), but once he turned to the writing
of realistic novels in the early 1860s, his name became widely
known throughout Great Britain and the U.S. Over the next
thirty years he wrote some fifty books, including, in addition
to the novels, more poetry, short stories, fantasies, sermons,
essays, and a full-length study of *Hamlet*. His influential

body of work placed him alongside the great Victorian men of letters, and his following was vast.

MacDonald died in 1905, and his reputation gradually declined in the twentieth century. Most of his books eventually went out of print as his name drifted from memory. A brief flurry of interest in his work was generated in 1924 at the centenary of his birth, resulting in several new editions of certain titles and the first major biography of his life, *George MacDonald and His Wife*, by his son Greville MacDonald.

Obscure though his name gradually became, however, MacDonald was read and revered by an impressive gallery of well-known figures, both in his own time and in the years since. A few of these include G. K. Chesterton (who called him "one of the three or four greatest men of the nineteenth century"), W. H. Auden (who said MacDonald was "one of the most remarkable writers of the nineteenth century"), Oswald Chambers ("How I love that man!"), and most notably C. S. Lewis.

Lewis acknowledged his spiritual debt to MacDonald as so great that he published an entire anthology of quotations by MacDonald in hopes of turning the public toward his spiritual mentor in large numbers. In the introduction to that volume Lewis wrote:

> I dare not say that he is never in error; but to speak plainly I know hardly any other writer who seems to be closer, or more continually close, to the Spirit of Christ Himself. . . . I have never concealed the fact that I regarded him as my master; indeed I fancy I have never written a book in which I did not quote from him.

Lewis's efforts, however, were but modestly successful, and for the most part only in literary circles. Notwithstanding Lewis's laudatory words, MacDonald's name continued to fall out of the public consciousness. By the 1960s, nearly all his work (except for a few stories and fairy tales) was out of print, though his inclusion, along with Lewis and his "inkling" friends, in the newly established Marion Wade Center at Wheaton College promised that he would not be forgotten.

A resurgence of interest, primarily in the United States, began to mount in the 1970s and 1980s, given initial impetus by the work of Wheaton professor Dr. Rolland Hein and then exploding into public view from the efforts of MacDonald redactor and biographer Michael Phillips. Phillips' work resulted in new generations of readers discovering anew the treasures in MacDonald's work and led to a renewed publication of MacDonald's books on a scale not seen since his own lifetime.

Michael Phillips (1946–), writer and novelist, is responsible for reawakening worldwide public interest in George Mac-Donald through publication of his edited and original editions of MacDonald's books.

Phillips first discovered MacDonald's work in the early 1970s. Dismayed to learn that all MacDonald's major fiction (as well as most other titles) was unavailable, Phillips embarked on an ambitious lifetime project to reintroduce the world to the remarkable author through many different means. Toward this end, he envisioned edited versions of MacDonald's dialect-heavy Scottish novels. The purpose of redacting these masterpieces would be a practical one—hopefully to interest a contemporary publisher (skeptical about a dense five-hundred-page Victorian tome) to publish and promote them, and also to make MacDonald's stories and spiritual wisdom available and compelling to a new and less literarily patient reading audience.

Phillips began his initial editing of MacDonald's *Malcolm* in the mid–1970s. Though it took five years and rejections by thirty houses to find a publisher to believe with him that MacDonald could speak to new generations, the eventual publication of his redacted edition of *Malcolm* was so successful and was received so enthusiastically by the reading public that it led to the eventual publication of eighteen redacted volumes that have to date sold over two million copies worldwide and have been translated into several foreign languages. The twentieth-century MacDonald renaissance had begun!

Over the next twenty years, Phillips expanded his efforts, producing original full-length editions of MacDonald's work to accompany the redacted novels, writing an acclaimed biography, *George MacDonald: Scotland's Beloved Storyteller*, producing a series of books and studies about MacDonald, and, like Lewis, compiling an anthology of quotations from MacDonald's titles (*Wisdom to Live By*).

During this time Phillips' own stature as one of the leading Christian novelists of the late twentieth century was also rising. He penned dozens of novels of his own that were as well received as had been his work with MacDonald. Phillips is today generally recognized as a man with a keen insight into MacDonald's heart and message. As his own volume of work reaches a stature of significance in its own right, he is regarded by many as the successor to MacDonald's vision and spiritual legacy for a new generation.

For more information about
George MacDonald and Michael Phillips, visit
www.macdonaldphillips.com.

Don't miss Michael Phillips' biography,
George MacDonald: Scotland's Beloved Storyteller,
as well as *Is Jesus Coming Back As Soon As We Think?*

For a complete listing of titles
by Michael Phillips and the availability of George MacDonald titles, both original and edited, write us at:

P. O. Box 7003
Eureka, CA 95502
U.S.A.